FATAL WORDS

Steven Cushing

FATAL WORDS

Communication Clashes and Aircraft Crashes

THE UNIVERSITY OF CHICAGO PRESS　　　*Chicago & London*

Steven Cushing is associate professor of computer science at Boston University.

THE UNIVERSITY OF CHICAGO PRESS, CHICAGO 60637
THE UNIVERSITY OF CHICAGO PRESS, LTD., LONDON
© 1994 by The University of Chicago
All rights reserved. Published 1994
Printed in the United States of America
02 01 00 99 98 97 96 95 94   1 2 3 4 5
ISBN: 0-226-13200-5 (cloth)

Library of Congress Cataloging-in-Publication Data

Cushing, Steven, 1948—
     Fatal words : communication clashes and aircraft crashes / by
   Steven Cushing.
         p.   cm.
     Includes index.
     1. Aeronautics—Terminology.   2. Airplanes—Piloting—Terminology.
   3. Air traffic control—Terminology.   4. Aeronautics—Accident
   investigation.   5. Communication of technical information.
     I. Title.
TL509.C87   1994
     363.12′418—cd20   93-24615
                                                                CIP

To the frogs who fly

Contents

Preface

In 1748 Julien Offroy de La Mettrie, a scientist-philosopher who foreshadowed modern robotics and artificial intelligence with what were then some good progressive ideas about human nature and its place in nature generally, still apparently felt comfortable expressing this disturbing sentiment: "It is not enough for a wise man to study nature and truth; he should dare state truth for the benefit of the few who are willing and able to think. As for the rest, voluntary slaves to prejudice, they can no more attain truth, than frogs can fly."[1] In the six years since I began the project reported here, as a summer faculty research fellow in human factors at NASA-Ames Research Center and Stanford University, I have presented the results on numerous occasions to "the few who are . . . able to think" about these things for a living: linguists, psychologists, cognitive scientists, and aviation specialists. My purpose in writing this book is to bring these results to the attention of those whom La Mettrie refers to as "the rest": the "frogs" who fly, who know people who fly, or who live in areas that airplanes fly over. Aviation safety is and will remain one of the central concerns of our time for anyone who lives on this planet. Ignorance of the role that miscommunication plays in undermining that safety is no more a result of "voluntary . . . prejudice" than is ignorance of any other issue about which the facts have yet to be made known.

The introduction summarizes the problem and gives some illustrative examples. The first four chapters, which constitute part 1, deal with problems of communication that are based more or less directly on language. The next four chapters, part 2, are concerned with other aspects of the communication situation with which language must interact. The final three chapters suggest some potential solutions, one of which is spelled out in more technical detail in the appendix.

Chapter 1 discusses problems that arise from characteristics of language itself: ambiguity, in which a word or phrase has more than one meaning; homophony, in which different words sound exactly or almost alike; peculiarities of punctuation or intonation, which can wreak havoc in even the simplest situations; and the complexity of speech acts, which correspond only in the most indirect ways to sentence or statement types.

Chapter 2 discusses problems that arise from the ways language can refer to the world: problems that arise from pronouns, which derive their usefulness precisely from being referentially indeterminate; problems that arise in determining who is being addressed in a particular communication; and problems that arise because aircraft must be handed off from one controller to another.

Chapter 3 discusses problems that arise from the inferences that are drawn in the course of communication: inferences that are implicit in the communicative situation; those that are invited by the use of particular words; those that a listener is forced to draw by being confronted with unfamiliar terminology; and false assumptions that arise from distractions and other sources.

Chapter 4 reviews the crucial notion of repetition and the ways it can succeed or fail in preventing or repairing communication foul-ups: the different kinds of repetition that can occur in linguistic communication; the full and partial readbacks that are required and discouraged, respectively, in the aviation protocol; the problems of repetition across more than one language; and the problems for interlocutory engagement when often-repeated formulations become ritualized.

Chapter 5 deals with problems that arise from the use of numbers, an aspect of language that serves as an interface with technical equipment: digit confusions and reversals; overlap of the value ranges of widely different aviation parameters; and the almost ubiquitous number problems that keep arising with altimeters.

Chapter 6 discusses the use and misuse of radios: when an aircraft lacks a radio and when an aircraft has a radio but the crew declines or forgets to use it.

Chapter 7 discusses how circumstances unrelated to communication nevertheless affect the outcome of a communicative exchange: problems can arise from distractions and fatigue, from impatience, from obstinacy and noncooperativeness, and from frivolousness or crew conflict.

Chapter 8 discusses more general problems that can arise in attempting to convey meaningful messages: when a message is not sent; when a message is sent but not heard; when a message is sent and heard but not understood; and when a message is sent, heard, and understood but not remembered.

Chapter 9 suggests some steps that can be taken immediately to ameliorate the problems discussed in the earlier chapters. Chapter 10 sketches out, for very long-term development, the requirements of an intelligent voice interface that could filter ongoing communications for potential confusions and provide real-time feedback and correction. Chapter 11 suggests, more realistically in the short term, the development of an error-resistant *visual* communication system that would enforce a standard protocol and supplement voice communications; it also describes a prototype visual touchscreen interface of the sort envisioned. Technical details of that prototype system are given in the appendix.

Readers who are interested exclusively in linguistic issues might want to skip part 2 and move directly to part 3, where those issues are taken up again. Most readers, however, will find the intervening chapters of interest, I think, because they place the linguistic issues within a broader communication perspective and underscore the seriousness of the aviation safety situation.

Readers with a computational bent will be especially interested in the appendix, which provides technical information on the system described in chapter 11. More such information can be obtained from the author at the following addresses:

Boston University
755 Commonwealth Avenue
Boston, MA 02215
USA

eMail: steve@bumeta.bu.edu
Telephone: (617) 524–1767

Some of the data presented here are taken from audiotapes of actual air-ground, pilot-controller dialogues recorded at a major airport, but most come from transcripts published in accident reports by the National Transportation Safety Board (NTSB) or from incident reports in the monthly bulletin *Callback*, published by the Aviation Safety Reporting System (ASRS) of NASA-Ames Research Center. These bulletins report a wide range of incidents, from simple anomalies to near misses, based on self-reports submitted by pilots, controllers, flight attendants, and sometimes even passengers. All identifying information is eliminated before publication, to ensure the anonymity and confidentiality that are necessary for the reporting system to work, but each case is carefully checked by ASRS investigators to determine the accuracy and general reliability of those self-reports. Identifying information has also been removed from the examples that are cited here from audiotapes. In such reports and transcriptions, capitalization, spelling, and so forth have been adjusted to conform to the main text of the book.

Acknowledgments

The work reported here was based in part on research supported by grants NGT 05-020-412 and NAG 2-564 from NASA-Ames Research Center, Mountain View, California, with Alfred T. Lee as technical monitor. I thank Dr. Lee for teaching me much of what I now know about aviation. I also thank Dr. William Reynard, director of the Aviation Safety and Reporting System (ASRS) and his assistant Patti Bergin for their helpfulness during the two summers I was an American Society for Engineering Education (ASEE) fellow at NASA-Ames; Dr. Daniel Bershader and his assistant Juanita Girand, who coordinated the ASEE program at Stanford University; and George Hagerty for his professional handling of contractual aspects of the visual interface project described in chapter 11. All opinions expressed in this book are my own. No NASA endorsement should be inferred.

Various aspects of this work have been published in articles cited in the notes. An earlier version of chapter 4 appears as a chapter in Barbara Johnstone, ed., *Repetition in Discourse: Interdisciplinary Perspectives* (Norwood, N.J.: Ablex, 1994), and that material is reprinted with the permission of Ablex Publishing Corporation. Some aspects have also been presented at conferences, including the annual meeting of the American Association for Applied Linguistics, San Francisco, California, December 1987; the Twenty-fourth International Congress of Psychology, Sydney, Australia, August 1988; the Conference on Repetition in Discourse: Interdisciplinary Perspectives, Texas A&M University, May 1990; the Third International Pragmatics Conference: The Interdependence of the Social and Cognitive Aspects of Language Use, Barcelona, July 1990; the Fourth International Aviation English Forum: Aviation English Standards, Paris, November 1991; the Fifteenth International Congress of Linguists, Quebec, August 1991; and the Fourth International Pragmatics Conference: Communication and Cognition in an Intercultural Context, Kobe, Japan, July 1993. I thank the organizers of these conferences for providing these opportunities to present my work and to get valuable feedback from interested listeners, and I thank Deans Robert Kruse and Allan Hershfield for helping to offset the cost of attending some of these conferences. Further thanks go to Andrew Allen, Herbert Armstrong, Martha Bean, Kip Becker, Alice Bennett, Hugh Bergeron, Bethany Dumas, Sharon Flank, Bruce Fraser, Susan Gass, Georgia Green, Geoffrey Huck, Barbara Johnstone, Carol Justus, James Kegl, Judy Kegl, Jay Keyser, Jacklin Kornfilt, George Lakoff, Charlotte Linde, Neil Norrick, Karen Peterson, Renate Rofske-Hofstrand, Ivan Sag, Muriel Vasconcellos, Benji Wald, and Stoyanka Tanya Zlateva for helpful comments of various sorts at different points in the work. Tanya Zlateva deserves special thanks for helping me think through the revisions for the final draft of the manuscript.

The system described in chapter 11 was developed, under my supervision, by Suzanne Artemieff, Robert Doutch, James Dowers, Gabe Elkin, Joanne Fantini, Boris Finkelstein, Michelle Guardabascio, Grant McCardell, Barry Paine, Alice Shafer, and Susan Willard as a part of their work as graduate students at Boston University. Suzanne Artemieff, Gabe Elkin, Barry Paine, and Alice Shafer helped in preparing the documentation for the system, which I have summarized here in the appendix. A database of relevant incidents culled from the NASA/ASRS monthly bulletin *Callback*, from which many of the examples here are taken, was compiled under my direction by two undergraduate students, Ann Sisco and David Ross.

Introduction

Language and Aviation Safety

The work reported here derives from a broader study of linguistic and cognitive factors in aviation safety involving analysis of the air-ground protocol language as defined in official
handbooks and as actually spoken by controllers and pilots,[1]
modeling of the cognitive processes that controllers use in lin-
ing up aircraft for landing,[2] and the design of experimental
tests to determine likely error types, their sources, and possible solutions.[3] In this book I focus on air-ground communication and, more specifically, on the problems that arise
from using voice-mediated language as the medium of that
communication.

Voice has a natural appeal as the preferred means of communication both among humans themselves and between
humans and machines, since it is the form of communication
people find most convenient. The complexity and flexibility of
natural language are problematic, however, because of the
confusions and misunderstandings that can readily arise as a
result of such specifically linguistic phenomena as ambiguity,
unclear reference, differences in intonation (or punctuation in
written language), implicit inference, and presupposition, as
well as from more general peculiarities of human interactions
face-to-face or over the radio. In particular, language-related
misunderstandings of various kinds have been a crucial contributing factor in aviation accidents and potential accidents.

For example, the accident at Los Rodeos airport, Tenerife,
the Canary Islands, on 27 March 1977 resulted in part from a
misunderstanding of the phrase *at takeoff*, which was used by
the flight crew to indicate that they were "in the *process* of taking off" but was understood by the tower controller as meaning "at the takeoff *point*."[4] The accident at John Wayne Orange
County Airport, Santa Ana, California, on 17 February 1981 re-

sulted in part from a misunderstanding of the verb *hold*, which always means "stop what you're doing" in standard aviation parlance but can mean "continue what you're doing" in idiomatic conversational English.[5] The accident that occurred at Miami International Airport on 29 December 1972 resulted in part from a misunderstanding of the reference of the word *things*, which the approach controller intended to refer to the aircraft's declining elevation, but which the crew took to refer to a nose-gear problem they had been preoccupied with.[6] The accident that occurred at Cove Neck, New York, on 25 January 1990 resulted in part from the fact that the copilot used the normal English phrase *running out of fuel* rather than the technical aviation term *emergency*, thereby failing to convey to the controller the intended degree of urgency.[7]

Many of the occurrences reviewed here can be attributed to a clash between individual cognitive and social interactive factors of language use. Individual cognitive factors are aspects of the communicative situation that have to do with the internal mental states or processes of individual speakers or hearers; social interactive factors are those aspects that have to do with the relation or interaction of two or more speakers or hearers. The former include such aspects as mental models of the world or of specific situations, judgments of the relative salience of various aspects of the world, preferred readings of words or phrases, assumed values or expectations, and systems of individual belief; the latter include such aspects as conventions of use, standardized definitions, officially prescribed protocols, cultural or ideological requirements, and relative status in a hierarchy of authority or command.

Much recent scientific linguistic research has involved arguments over which sort of factor is most important in language, but there appears to be an emerging consensus that both are indispensable. Adequate formal models of language use will have to contain parameters representing the mutual relations of these factors. More generally, theories of individual cognitive phenomena must make reference to parameters whose values are set by social interactions,[8] and theories of social interactive phenomena must refer to parameters whose values are set by the cognitive particularities of the individual minds that participate in those phenomena.[9] As I have argued elsewhere, the facts of aviation communication appear to bear this out.[10] Like meaningful human language use generally, aviation communication typically involves a complex interplay of both of these sorts of factors.[11] If the two sorts of factors fail to match in the ways they are supposed to, the result can be disaster.

For example, investigators determined the probable cause of the accident that occurred at Monroe County Airport, Rochester, New York, on 9 July 1978 to be "*the captain's complete lack of awareness* of airspeed, vertical speed, and aircraft performance," along with "*the first officer's failure to provide required callouts* that might have alerted the captain to the airspeed and sink rate deviations" (emphasis added). In other words, the accident resulted from the captain's cognitive state, his lack of awareness of the values of essential quantities he should have been made aware of through a linguistic social interaction—the callouts required from the first officer. If the failure to provide required callouts resulted, in turn, from a feeling of discomfort or intimidation on the part of the first officer in response to his relation to the captain in the authority hierarchy, then that further clash of cognitive and social factors also contributed to this miscommunication. As a result, "the aircraft overran the end of the runway, . . . crossed a drainage ditch and came to rest 728 feet past the end of the runway threshold." Damage to the aircraft was substantial, though there was no fire, and "one passenger was injured seriously."[12]

Similarly, investigators determined the probable cause of the accident that occurred at Portland (Oregon) International Airport on 28 December 1978 to be "*the failure of the captain* to monitor properly the aircraft's fuel state and *to properly respond to* the low fuel state and *the crew member's advisories regarding fuel state*," a failure resulting from "*preoccupation with a landing-gear malfunction* and preparations for a possible landing emergency." "Contributing to the accident was the failure of the other two flight crew members *either to fully comprehend* the criticality of the fuel state *or to successfully communicate their concern to the captain*" (emphasis added). Here we have an interesting reblending of aspects already seen in the examples cited earlier. As in the Cove Neck accident, the fuel is low and the other crew members realize this; but this time, as in the Miami example, the captain is too preoccupied with a landing-gear problem to notice. In contrast to the Monroe County example, the crew members do provide the captain with appropriate advisories; but as in the Miami case, these are not of such a nature as to prompt the necessary corrective action. As in the Cove Neck accident, the crew members appear, from the investigator's report, to have said *something*, but not something that would convey the proper degree of urgency.

The captain's social obligation to respond appropriately to the linguistic productions of interlocutors was undermined by his cognitive preoccupation. Conversely, those interlocutors failed to execute successfully their social obligation to communicate their message in a form that would succeed in altering the captain's cognitive state, perhaps because of their own cognitive failure "to fully comprehend the criticality" of the situation. In the end, the aircraft "crashed into a wooded populated area . . . during an approach to the . . . airport," resulting in the aircraft's complete destruction. "Of the 181 passengers and 8 crew members aboard, 8 passengers, the flight engineer, and a flight attendant were killed and 21 passengers and 2 crew members were injured seriously."[13]

These examples are representative of a wide range of fatal or near-fatal aviation accidents and near accidents in which language misunderstandings or omissions or communication confusion of various other sorts have played a contributing or even central role. Many such examples are presented in this book, and some potential solutions to the problem they pose are suggested.

Part I

Language-Based
Communication Problems

Problems of Language

The Tenerife and John Wayne accidents both involved ambiguities, as was noted in the introduction, the former in the preposition *at*, and the latter in the verb *hold*. In general, ambiguity is the presence of two or more meanings in a word, phrase, sentence, or passage. For example, the subtitle (1) of this book can be interpreted either as a noun phrase, with the adjectives *communication* and *aircraft* modifying the respective nouns *clashes* and *crashes*, or as a sentence, with the nouns *communication* and *aircraft* serving as the subjects of the verbs *clashes* and *crashes*.

(1)   Communication Clashes and Aircraft Crashes

In the first case it has the meaning (2a), and in the second it has the meaning (2b).

(2a)   [This book deals with] clashes related to communication
            and crashes related to aircraft.
(2b)   When instances of communication clash, instances of
            aircraft crash.

Sentence (3), a classic example in the linguistic literature,[1] can mean either (4a) or (4b), depending on whether the phrase *flying planes* is intended to mean planes themselves that are flying or the activity of making planes fly.

(3)   Flying planes can be dangerous.

(4a)   Planes that are flying can be dangerous.
(4b)   To fly planes can be dangerous.

Sentence (5) can mean either (6a) or (6b), depending on whether the phrase *the shooting of officers* is intended to mean the way officers shoot, as in a report that evaluates their skill, or the fact that officers are shot, as in a conversation about fragging or the treatment of prisoners in wartime.

(5)   The shooting of officers is nothing to write home about.

(6a)   The shooting done by officers is nothing to write home about.

(6b)   That officers are shot is nothing to write home about.

In the (a) readings of (3) and (5), the planes or officers are the agents of the flying or shooting, those which or who perform the indicated act, whereas in the (b) readings they are its recipients, those on which or whom the indicated act is performed. Furthermore, in (1), (3), and (5), the phrases or sentences themselves contain no overt indication of the intended interpretation. This can be determined only (if at all: for the subtitle [1], both readings are appropriate) by examining the context in which the phrase or sentence is uttered or written.

Each of these ambiguities is of a structural nature, since different meanings emerge from differences in how the grammar of the phrase or sentence is analyzed, as the contrast between (a) and (b) in each case shows. However, the sentences also contain lexical ambiguities, in which different meanings emerge as a result of there being more than one meaning for an individual word. Sentence (3) can be uttered with its (4a) reading to quiet a rowdy woodworking class, if *planes* is intended to mean carpentry tools rather than aircraft, and it can be uttered with its (4b) reading to express a reluctance to travel, if *flying* is intended to mean being a passenger rather than a pilot. Sentence (5) can be uttered with its (6a) reading as an evaluation of the officers' skills at billiards and with either its (6a) or (6b) reading as an evaluation of photography.

Ambiguity is an ever-present source of potential air-ground misunderstandings. For example, pilots use the term (7) for both (8a) and (8b).[2]

(7)   PD

(8a)   Pilot's discretion
(8b)   Profile descent

An instructor reports responding to the Tower calling traffic by saying (9a), with the intended meaning (9b), but being interpreted by his student as meaning that the instructor was now flying the aircraft.[3]

(9a)   I got it.
(9b)   I see the traffic.

In a similar incident, a copilot reports calling that the landing field was in sight by saying (10), with the result that the flying pilot let go of the controls.[4]

(10)   I've got it.

Sentence (11) is interpreted sometimes as meaning that "the pilot maintains the heading indicated when lined up on the extended center line of the runway" and sometimes as meaning that "the pilot takes a heading after liftoff to keep the aircraft traveling on the extended line of the runway."

(11)   Maintain runway heading.

In some situations this difference can lead to a conflict between aircraft during a crosswind situation after takeoff.[5]
    At an airport at which Local Control and Ground Control were combined, a construction vehicle, B1, called (12).

(12)   At the localizer road to proceed to the ramp.

A controller, knowing that B1 had called but not sure what the request had been, replied (13) and then proceeded to talk to aircraft while waiting for a reply.

(13)   B1, Ground, go ahead.

B1 misinterpreted the phrase *go ahead* as referring to his driving, rather than his speaking, and was halfway down his normal route of travel before the controller realized what had happened.[6]
    Looking more closely at the dialogue that took place in the Tenerife case, shown here in (14), we see that misunderstanding the ambiguous phrase *at takeoff* in line 1706:09.61 as meaning (15a), rather than (15b), which was what the pilot intended, prevented the Tower from telling the pilot to abort his takeoff.

(14)
1705:44.6 KLM 4805:   The KLM *four* eight zero *five* is now ready for takeoff and we are waiting for our ATC clearance (1705:50.77).

1705:53.41 Tower: KLM eight *seven* zero five you are cleared to the
Papa Beacon, climb to and maintain flight level nine zero, right
turn after takeoff, proceed with heading four zero until intercepting
the three two five radial from Las Palmas VOR (1706:08.09).
1706:09.61 KLM 4805:   Ah—roger sir, we are cleared to the Papa
Beacon, flight level nine zero until intercepting the three two five.
We are now at takeoff (1706:17.79).
1706:18.19 Tower: OK . . . Stand by for takeoff, I will call you
(1706:21.79).
[*Note:* A squeal starts at 1706:19.39 and ends at 1706:22.06.]
[PAA: And we're still taxiing down the runway the Clipper one
seven three six (1706:23.6).]
1706:21.92 PAA 1736:   Clipper one seven three six (1706:23.39).
1706:25.47 Tower: Ah—Papa Alpha one seven three six report the
runway clear (1706:28.89).
1706:29.59 PAA 1736:   OK, will report when we're clear (1706:30.69).
1706:61 [*sic*].69 Tower: Thank you.
1706:50: COLLISION: KLM on takeoff run collides with PAA on
ground.

Los Rodeos Airport, Tenerife, Canary Islands, 27 March 1977

(15a)   waiting at the takeoff point
(15b)   already on the takeoff roll

This misunderstanding resulted, in turn, from a prior confusion as to exactly what the clearance (16) in line 1705:53.41 had
been, because telling the pilot what to do *after takeoff* does not
necessarily constitute giving the pilot permission *to take off*.

(16)   you are cleared to the Papa Beacon, climb to and maintain
flight level nine zero, right turn after takeoff

The KLM pilot interprets the clearance as permission to fly to
the Papa Beacon, but the Tower appears to have intended it
as permission to fly to that beacon only after having received
further clearance to leave the ground. The subsequent collision
with another aircraft that was still on the runway resulted in
the loss of 583 lives, the worst accident in aviation history. The
use of alternative unambiguous phrases for the clearance and
the takeoff announcement would have enabled the controller
to advise some action that might have averted the collision or
prevented the takeoff roll in the first place.[7]

Ambiguity in the verb *hold* in lines 0134:16 and 0134:18 of the
dialogue in (17) contributed to the accident at John Wayne.

(17)
0133:11 Tower: Air California *three* thirty *six*, you're cleared to land.
0133:33 Tower: Air California *nine* thirty *one* let's do it taxi into
position and hold,   be ready.
0133:37 AC 931:   Nine thirty one's ready.
0133:52 Tower: Air Cal nine thirty one traffic clearing at the end, clear
for takeoff sir,   Boeing seven thirty seven a mile and a half final.
0133:57 AC 931:   In sight we're rolling.
0134:13 Tower: OK Air Cal *three thirty six,* go around three thirty six,
go around.
(0134:16 AC 336 captain: *Can we* hold, ask him if we can—hold.)
0134:18 Tower: Air Cal *nine thirty one* if you can just go ahead and
hold—.
0134:21 AC 336:   *Can we* land Tower?
0134:22 Tower: Behind you Air Cal nine thirty one *just* abort.
0134:25 Tower: Air Cal three thirty six, please *go around* sir traffic is
going to abort   on the departure.
(0134:27 AC 336 captain: Gear up.)
0134:36: IMPACT: Aircraft lands with gear retracted.

John Wayne Orange County Airport, Santa Ana, California, 17
February 1981

In aviation parlance, *hold* always means to stop what you are
now doing and thus to go around in a landing situation; but in
everyday English it can also mean to continue what you are
now doing and thus to land in such a situation. In fact, the 336
officer seems to interpret it in exactly the latter way at 0134:21,
when he asks for permission to land in response to the captain's intracockpit instruction to ask for permission to hold. In
effect, the captain and officer slip momentarily, perhaps inadvertently, from the technical jargon they are supposed to be
speaking to the colloquial dialect they most likely speak normally, a phenomenon that linguists refer to as code switching.
The resulting confusion led to Air California 336's landing with
its gear retracted, having finally decided to go around, but too
late actually to do so. This resulted in thirty-four injuries, four
of them classified as serious, and the complete destruction
of the aircraft by impact and postimpact fire. Of course the
accident could have been avoided altogether had the pilot
simply followed instructions and gone around when he was
first told to.[8]

HOMOPHONY

The ambiguity-induced confusion in the John Wayne accident in (17) is compounded by the fact that the two aircraft in question have barely distinguishable call signs, with Air Call three *thirty* six being told to go *around* in line 0134:13 and Air Cal nine *thirty* one being told to go *ahead* in line 0134:18, just five seconds later. This illustrates the similar confusion-inducing phenomena of homophony and, more commonly, near homophony, which consist in different words or phrases sounding exactly or nearly alike.

In the words of one controller, "Sometimes, in response to a request from another controller, a fellow might say [(18)]."

(18)   I'll let you know.

"About every other Tuesday this sound like [(19)]."[9]

(19)   Let him go.

A pilot reports that ten years earlier, when he was "practicing short field landings in a small airplane, the instructor said [(20)], meaning to reduce to zero as we flared."

(20)   Last of the power.

However, the pilot thought the instructor had said (21), "fearing an imminent stall—result: confusion and rather longer landing."[10]

(21)   Blast of power.

Sentence (22) is ambiguous because *left* can mean either the speaker's left or the hearer's left; but further confusion is also possible because *left* sounds very much like *west*.[11]

(22)   Pass to the left of the tower.

An aircraft that received the clearance (23) replied with (24a), which, "given any crew or ATC distraction . . . could be easily misinterpreted as" (24b), "a common, though nonstandard response to takeoff clearance."[12]

(23)   Position and hold.

(24a)   On the hold.
(24b)   On the go.

A pilot who "was observed on radar to be somewhat higher than called for in the procedure, and flying in the wrong direction" turned out to have misheard a clearance for (25a) as a clearance for (25b).

(25a)   a Maspeth climb
(25b)   a massive climb

"Maspeth is a fix in the New York metropolitan area," but the pilot was "unfamiliar with the local geography."[13]

An outbound pilot who was told to receive his clearance from the Center when he was (26a) misheard this as (26b) and proceeded with his takeoff, "rather than contacting Center on the ground—which I did not realize I could do."

(26a)   on the deck
(26b)   off the deck

He consequently found himself "on the same localizer in opposite directions" as an inbound aircraft.[14] In another incident, a wide-body air carrier A landed on runway 22L and was advised to taxi inbound and hold short of 22R. Holding short of 22R, the captain asked (27), to which the controller responded (28).

(27)   May we cross?

(28)   Hold short.

A then crossed the departure runway with wide-body carrier B starting its departure roll. Consequently A cleared 22R approximately thirty seconds before B reached the intersection, with no evasive action taken by either aircraft. When asked why he had crossed the runway, the A captain explained that he had heard (28) as (29).[15]

(29)   Oh sure.

A pilot reports having first thought he had been given the clearance (30a) and then realizing he had actually been given the opposite clearance (30b).[16]

(30a)   Cleared for takeoff and cleared into the TCA.
(30b)   Cleared for takeoff and remain clear of TCA.

A captain who thought that Departure Control had cleared him to 11,000 feet and that his copilot had confirmed this with

(31a) found out later that the controller had actually been pointing out traffic at 11,000 feet and that the copilot had actually said (31b) in reference to the traffic.[17]

(31a)   Cleared to eleven thousand.
(31b)   He's clear at eleven thousand.

Another pilot reports misconstruing (32a) and (32b).

(32a)   Slow to 170, descent in four miles.
(32b)   Slow to 170, descend to four.

"At 9,500 the controller advised us to maintain 10,000."[18]
    In an aircraft "being vectored for a landing on 27L and maintaining [an] assigned altitude of 10,000 feet," the flying captain thought he heard the copilot say (33a), took this to mean (33b), and started to descend.

(33a)   Cleared to seven.
(33b)   Cleared to seven thousand feet.

At 9,500 feet the copilot said they should really be at 10,000, and the controller confirmed this but then cleared them to 7,000. Upon reflection the captain realized that the copilot's (33a) had really meant "that our assigned runway was TWO seven—Not that we were cleared TO seven [thousand feet]."[19] Similar confusions between the identical sounding *to* and *two* almost led to a midair collision in the incident in (34)[20] and did lead to a fatal accident in the incident in (35).[21]

---

(34)
1. Departure Control gives a clearance heard as "Climb two five zero."
2. Copilot repeats that clearance and dials 25,000 into the autopilot.
3. Pilot notices traffic 1,500 feet above and resets dial to descend to 5,000.

    Controller: *To* ⇒ Copilot: *Two*

---

(35)
1. Controller clears the aircraft to descend "two four zero zero."
2. Pilot reads clearance back as "OK. Four zero zero."
3. Aircraft descends to 400 feet rather than the appropriate altitude of 2,400 feet.

    Controller: 2,400 ⇒ Pilot: [*To*] 400

PUNCTUATION AND INTONATION

Similar sorts of confusion can occur from mistakes in punctuation, as illustrated by (36), in which (a) and (b) are pronounced exactly alike. The presence of an apostrophe in (36a) but not (36b) drastically alters the sense of the statement, since *calling someone's name* is different from *calling someone names*.

(36a)   The flight attendant stood by the door and called the
          passengers' names as they arrived.
(36b)   The flight attendant stood by the door and called the
          passengers names as they arrived.

The action described in (36a) might well be one of the flight attendant's job responsibilities, but the action described in (36b), which differs in its written description by only a single blotch of ink, could well lead to job termination.

In spoken language the same kind of difference can occur in intonation. Stressing the word *flying* in (3) gives it the meaning (37), in which *flying* identifies the planes by the purpose for which they are intended, instead of either of the meanings in (4).

(37)   Planes that are intended for flying can be dangerous.

In the dialogue (38), from the movie *Brubaker*, the stressed words are spoken with lower pitch (↓) in the first sentence and higher pitch (↑) in the third, with the result that the two sentences, with the same words in the same order, have exactly opposite meanings, one disparaging and the other complimentary.

(38)   That's a <u>hell</u> ↓ of an <u>idea</u> ↓ ! What was that?! I say, that's a
          <u>hell</u> ↑ of an <u>idea</u> ↑ !

The classic dialogue (39–40) from a Three Stooges film is based on a deliberate confusion between (39) and (41), which differ only in the length of the pause between *think* and *I*.

(39)   I don't think! I know!

(40)   I don't think you know either!

(41)   I don't think I know.

Opposite meanings of a sentence can often be distinguished easily in speech by changing the pitch of stressed words, as indicated here for (38) by the ad hoc symbols ↓ and ↑ , but there is no normal punctuation device for indicating this contrast in standard writing conventions.

In a real example with potentially disastrous consequences, while checking out a pilot in a small airplane, an experienced flight instructor reports noticing considerable power on just before touching down. He thought he said (42a), but he was interpreted by the pilot as having said (42b), which normally differs in pronunciation only in the placement of the pause and whether *on* is stressed.[22]

(42a)   Back—on the power.
(42b)   Back on—the power.

SPEECH ACTS

Phrases can also be ambiguous with respect to the speech acts they are used to perform, such as statements, questions, requests, promises, and the like. A sentence like (43), for example, can be uttered to describe the temperature in the room, to request that the window be opened, to express discomfort, or to inquire about the comfort of the addressee, with different responses being appropriate in each case.

(43)   Gee, it's getting really warm in here.

A pilot who had been issued (44) and who had then acknowledged (45) was observed descending through 6,800 feet.

(44)   traffic at ten o'clock, three miles, level at 6,000, to pass
         under you

(45)   We have him.

Asked "if he was maintaining 7,000 as instructed," he "stated he read back 6,000." The pilot had misconstrued the phrase (46a) imperatively, as an instruction for himself, meaning (46b), rather than understanding it declaratively, as it was intended, as an assertion about his traffic, meaning (46c).[23]

(46a)   level at 6,000
(46b)   [Descend to and remain] level at 6,000.
(46c)   [The traffic is] level at 6,000.

The misunderstanding of the clearance in (14) may also have involved a speech-act confusion between an instruction for later and a permission for now, but it may simply have been an ambiguity in the content of a permission.

2

Problems of Reference

UNCERTAIN REFERENCE

Sometimes ambiguity arises because of uncertain reference, in which there is a degree of indeterminacy as to just who or what is meant by a pronoun or pronounlike expression. Sentence (47) can have any of the meanings in (48), depending on who is flying or going to fly at the time the sentence is uttered, as well as on the gender of the pilot.

(47)   She told the pilot her flight would be late.

(48a)   She told the pilot her own flight would be late.
(48b)   She told the pilot the pilot's flight would be late.
(48c)   She told the pilot someone else's flight would be late.

The pronoun *it* in (49) can be referring to the state or experience of being a pilot, if the husband is unskilled in piloting airplanes; to the fact of his wife's being a pilot, if he thinks she is a flight attendant or traveling salesperson; or to something else entirely, such as a burglary in which flight-related evidence is found unexpectedly at the scene of the crime.

(49)   His wife is a pilot, but he doesn't know anything about it.

In (50) and (51), uncertainty arises because of a difference between standard textbook grammar and actual colloquial usage.

(50)   The pilot was late for the flight, which caused much comment.

(51)   He has vetoed sixteen bills, all of which have been sustained.[1]

By standard grammar the relative pronoun *which* must have an earlier occurring noun phrase as its antecedent, so it is the flight that causes the comment in (50) and sixteen bills that have been sustained in (51), since those are the only earlier nonhuman noun phrases that occur in the sentences. In actual usage, however, it is the lateness of the pilot that is understood as causing the comment and the vetoes of the bills that have been sustained, even though *the lateness* and *the vetoes* do not explicitly appear as noun phrases. This kind of clash between textbook grammar and colloquial usage can be especially troublesome for people who learn English as a second language as adults, as do many foreign pilots and controllers. Uncertainty about the reference of the pronouns in such sentences can lead to confusion as to just what meaning the sentence is intended to express.

One of two fighters on instrument route developed mechanical problems and stated (52a), after which the controller then issued an IFR clearance, to which the aircraft replied (52b).

(52a)   We need a clearance back to base.
(52b)   We are in a left turn and we are climbing to 17,000.

The controller interpreted *we* as meaning that both aircraft were returning to home station, when in fact only the lead aircraft wanted to return, a misunderstanding resulting from an uncertainty in the reference of the pronoun *we*. "The wing man continued on the original IFR clearance and completed out the military route through the airspace of two centers."[2]

Similar confusion can occur with adjectives. An aircraft that "had landed on runway 15 [and] slowed almost to a stop abeam taxiway Mike" was then told (53) by the Tower but was uncertain what was being referred to by *next*.

(53)   Taxi to the next and hold short of 21.

"To get to 'the next' taxiway we would have to cross 21 prior to reaching taxiway Foxtrot. Or by 'the next' did he mean runway 21?" Fortunately "there was no conflict that resulted."[3]

Unfortunately, uncertainty about the reference of the indefinite noun *things* in line 2341:40 of the dialogue in (54) contributed directly to the Miami accident, as noted in the introduction.[4]

(54)
2334:05 EAL 401:   Ah, Tower this is Eastern, ah four zero one, it looks like we're gonna have to circle, we don't have a light on our nose gear yet.

2334:14 Tower: Eastern four oh one heavy, roger, pull up, climb
straight ahead to two thousand, go back to approach control, one
twenty eight six.

2334:21 EAL 401:   Okay, going up to two thousand, one twenty eight
six.

2335:09 EAL 401:   All right, ah, approach control, Eastern four zero
one, we're right over the airport here and climbing to two thousand
feet, in fact, we've just reached two thousand feet and we've got to
get a green light on our nose gear.

2336:27 MIA Approach Control: Eastern four oh one, turn left heading
three zero zero.

2338:46 EAL 401:   Eastern four oh one'll go ah, out west just a little
further *if we can here and, ah, see if we can get this light to come on
here.*

2341 Second officer within cockpit: I can't see it, it's pitch dark and *I
throw the little light, I get, ah, nothing.*

2341:40 MIA App Con: Eastern, ah, four oh one *how are things
comin' along* out there?

2341:44 EAL 401:   OK, we'd like to turn around and come, come back
in.

2341:47 MIA App Con: Eastern four oh one turn left heading one eight
zero.

2342:12: IMPACT: Aircraft crashes into the Everglades.

Miami International Airport, 29 December 1972

The approach controller used *things* to refer to the aircraft's apparent decline in elevation, which he had seen indicated on radar and wanted to check with the crew, but the crew appears to
have taken it to refer to a nose-gear problem that they had been
preoccupied with and had just informed the controller about.
They were unaware of the decline in elevation precisely because of this preoccupation. When the crew responds with
(55), the controller erroneously concludes that the decline in
elevation is under control, even though, in fact, the crew has
not a clue that the elevation is even an issue.

(55)   Okay.

The aircraft subsequently crashed into the Everglades, resulting in 101 deaths.[5]

UNCERTAIN ADDRESSEE

Confusion over the identity of the intended addressee can interfere with efficient information transfer as, for example, in the incident in (56).[6]

---

(56)
1. Aircraft A is "maintaining flight level 250," after having "requested lower and been told descent would be forthcoming."
2. Center issues a descent clearance for aircraft A, but this is "not received or acknowledged" by A.
3. Aircraft B *answers the descent clearance intended for A* and begins descent.
4. Aircraft A, "eastbound and about to start a right turn," hears controller tell another aircraft: "Maintain 260, turn left account for traffic to the right."
5. Aircraft A sees "an aircraft apparently southbound" out the left side and decides to take "a right turn to SSW."
6. Aircraft B reports to Center: "Traffic in sight."
7. Aircraft A is issued (and receives) clearance: "Descend on present heading."

Pilot Answers Someone Else's Descent Clearance

A pilot reports the following startling occurrence (emphasis added):

> VVXY was the aircraft ahead of us on departure. Our flight number was VWXY. After our takeoff, ATC requested VVXY to turn to 360 degrees; then issued climb clearance to 9,000 feet with only the "XY" heard. (The first two digits were blocked out.) *No company prefix was used with the flight number.* From our 250 degree heading we started a climbing right turn and requested confirmation of the 360 degree heading. We were told to maintain 250. Clearance to VVXY was then given to head 360 degrees and climb to 9000 feet. (*No company prefix.*) We immediately returned to our 250 degree heading and descended back to 2,000 feet after reaching 2,800 feet in our climbing turn. . . . The controller continued to issue clearances *not using company prefixes* until we left the frequency.[7]

Another pilot, who "had received and verified a clearance to 3,000," was told by Approach Control to stop his descent at 10,000 feet because the clearance had really been intended for "a commuter on the frequency with the same flight number." He speculates that "the company name could have been garbled. . . . Maybe there was a little 'hearback' problem, with the controller not catching the full ID during the clearance readback."[8]

Such garblings occur frequently, according to one pilot, because of

> the need for speed—hence the rapid-fire "push-the-button-to-speak" syndrome we all tend to fall into. I see/hear a very pronounced tendency toward clipping the first half-word from many controller transmissions. The switch not closing quickly enough or the transmitter not at peak power when the first word is uttered can have very much to do with who is going to be listening to the remainder of the first phrase. A missing identifier causes many repeats every hour of every day.[9]

A controller agrees:

> Yes, controllers do talk fast. We are using equipment older than most of today's work force and it engages a lot slower than our brains. It's hard—very hard— to wait after we key the mike before we speak. With today's hub system there are times when "nonstop" talking isn't enough.[10]

Furthermore, "there is . . . a time lag between the keying of a mike and the transmitter's actual output. Many controllers use a foot treadle to bring alive a boom mike; pilots either press the mike button or, in many cases, another button on the yoke."[11] As another pilot points out,

> Another problem in communications . . . is that of the controller or pilot who treats the mike button like a hair trigger on a rifle. Most of the newer equipment has automatic squelch controls. This . . . removes some operations errors, but most people do not understand that there is a time delay between the time that a receiver receives a carrier frequency and when it automatically opens the squelch so that the audio can go through. Often first words of a sentence are missed or misunderstood, and it is due to impatience in starting talking.[12]

Another pilot "cruising at 16,000 feet MSL," after hearing and acknowledging a clearance "for a descent to 11,000 feet MSL," reached 14,500 feet before being informed "that the clearance was for another aircraft."[13]

Similar confusions can also arise from frequency mix-ups. Four cockpit crewmen confirm hearing and acknowledging a clearance to flight level 240 on westbound departure control frequency XXX.4 and then being told on eastbound frequency XXX.0 that "no such clearance had been issued."[14] An "air carrier pilot inbound to a busy airport [but] unable to get a word in because of heavy chatter . . . elected to take a wave-off" when traffic Approach Control had told him to follow began turning off. Upon announcing this intention to the Tower, he was told, "You are talking to the wrong tower."[15] A "small aircraft had a near miss with a light twin on final for ABC airport" because "the pilot . . . changed to what he thought was the ABC local frequency for clearance . . . [but] had in fact changed to XYZ's local frequency and was cleared through *their* ATA" (Airport Traffic Area) instead.[16]

UNCLEAR HAND-OFFS

Uncertainty about just who or what is being referred to can also be brought about by unclear hand-offs, much as the hand-offs in (54) exacerbate the uncertain reference in (54), line 2341:40. In another incident, a new controller noticed aircraft A and B merging as A was leaving flight level 348. The pilot of A had "advised climbing to FL 370" when he reported in, and the controller at that time had "acknowledged but did not verify the assigned altitude." The new controller had been told by his predecessor that "aircraft A had been stopped at FL 330," but "tape recordings indicate that A was never recleared to FL 330."[17]

In a similar incident, when "aircraft A called stating he was on frequency at 6,000," the controller, "assuming it was his initial call-up . . . gave him the beacon code on the flight progress strip. A few seconds later he acquired about one mile behind aircraft B." The system error investigation found later that (1) "the relieved controller had been in contact with A and amended his clearance assigning a heading of 090 degrees," (2) *"he had forgotten about A at the time of relief,"* and (3) "the aircraft had not been assigned his correct code which would have resulted in autoacquisition."[18]

"An instrument student [120 hours total time]" had "filed a

VFR flight plan" and then "contacted ATC and filed an instrument flight plan" while "at 3,000 feet between cloud layers . . . when the layers of clouds started to merge." He was then passed from Center to Approach Control to the Tower to Approach again, the controllers all telling him to maintain VFR with various climb and descend clearances, even though he was in IMC the whole time.[19]

Problems of Inference

In implicit inference, a hearer derives meaning from a sentence that is not clearly explicit in its words or grammar. The first clause of (57) makes a favorable statement about the passengers and the second makes no reference to the passengers at all, but the two clauses taken together as a single sentence make a clearly disparaging statement about the passengers.

(57)   No doubt the passengers are honest, but I wouldn't leave my wallet lying around.

Both sentences of (58) make clearly positive statements, but the effect of the entire utterance is equally clearly negative.

(58)   The flight was just wonderful. The copilot was awake the whole time.

In both (57) and (58), a meaning is inferred from the juxtaposition of two clauses or sentences that is opposite or irrelevant to the explicit meaning of either clause or sentence individually. Typically in such cases, the meaning inferred from the juxtaposition is pejorative, as in these examples, though the individual clauses or sentences are not.

Implicit inferences can also be induced by the contrast between a sentence's grammatical structure and that of a sentence with which it is not juxtaposed. In syntactic misdirection an incorrect meaning is inferred for a sentence because the first part looks syntactically like a different sentence from what the rest of it really turns out to be. The term *garden-path* is often used to refer to such sentences, since they mislead the hearer "down the garden path" as to what is going on. Sentence (59a) is perfectly normal, but (59b) seems bizarre until one realizes that *taxied*, the verb in (59a), is a participle modifying *plane* in (59b), leaving further room in the latter for its actual verb *crashed*.

(59a)   The plane taxied past the tower.
(59b)   The plane taxied past the tower   crashed.

The meaning of (59b) is the same as that of (60a), more explicitly spelled out in (60b), because English allows generally for the optional omission of the relative phrase *that is* (or in this case the past tense, *that was*) when followed by a modifying multiword phrase.

(60a)   The plane (that was) taxied past the tower   crashed.
(60b)   The plane   crashed.
               ⇓   ⇑
          —I mean the one that was taxied past the tower—

The misleading part of the misunderstood sentence need not itself be a complete sentence. The meaning of (61a) is straightforward, but (61b) is confusing because *sent*, the verb in (61a), is a participle in (61b), which also contains the further verb *was*.

(61a)   The clearance sent the plane   on its way.
(61b)   The clearance sent the plane   wasn't heard.

In this case, in contrast to (60), the confusion is caused not because the first part of (61b) is a sentence in its own right, but because it has a preferred analysis, upon first hearing, as the beginning of the different sentence (61a). For (61b) to be meaningful, we must infer the implicit presence of the omitted components that are indicated in (62a).

(62a)   The clearance (that was) sent (to) the plane wasn't heard.
(62b)   *The clearance (that was) sent (to) the plane on its way.

The same inference applied to (61a) produces the meaningless (and therefore *-marked) nonsentence (62b).

   The misunderstanding in (42) is an example of syntactic misdirection, with the two different analyses normally distinguished by the placement of the pause. Stressing *on* groups it phrasally with *Back*, whereas leaving it unstressed groups it phrasally with *the power*, with consequent placement of the pause in each case.

LEXICAL INFERENCE

Implicit inferences can sometimes be induced through the use of a single word, especially if that word has a presupposition, an aspect of meaning that prevents a question in *yes/no* form from having a simple *yes/no* answer. Answering (63) with either yes or no equally commits the responder to an implicit admission that the pilot has been drinking.

(63)   Is the pilot still hung over?

Only an explicit denial of that presupposition, going well beyond a simple yes or no, as in (64), will suffice to counter that tacit admission.

(64)   Just a minute! What do you mean? The pilot wasn't drinking!

Answering (65) with (66) still leaves the impression that (67) is true, an implicit inference that can be countered only with something like (68).

(65)   Are all crew members present?

(66)   No, not all crew members are present.

(67)   Some crew members are present.

(68)   No. In fact, no crew members are present.

Though (69) and (70) appear to be opposites, both grant the presupposition (71), which can be denied only by something like (72), which looks like, but is not, the denial of (73).

(69)   Only the pilot knows what's going on.

(70)   Not only the pilot knows what's going on.

(71)   The pilot knows what's going on.

(72)   Not even the pilot knows what's going on.

(73)   Even the pilot knows what's going on.

Each of (63), (65), and (69) contains a word—*still*, *all*, and *only*, respectively—whose semantic effect is preserved even when the sentence appears to be negated.[1] In (72), *not even* has the effect of denying the presupposition (71) of (69) and (70), even though *even* itself in (73) has the very different presupposition (74).

(74)   That the pilot knows what's going on is surprising.

Dangerous inferences can also be drawn—and in fact are drawn, in aviation settings—from the use of such words as *expect* and *anticipate*, because of the time lag and indefiniteness that such words imply. An aircraft "cruising at flight level 310 . . . asked for FL 240 due to moderate chop" and was told to "expect it in twenty miles." After a flight attendant "stuck her head through the door" to discuss a recurring temperature problem, the captain mistook the first officer's readback of a heading 280 clearance as a clearance to FL 280 and began a descent. The captain erroneously inferred a flight level clearance from what was actually a readback to a heading clearance, because a flight level clearance, with a very similar number, was what he had been told to expect.[2]

Inference from *expect* had a different kind of consequence when a crew, "prior to arrival at the VOR . . . was told to 'expect' 210 knots at four miles." The copilot, "flying, missed that call due to descending and thunderstorm avoidance." When they arrived at the VOR, "the captain said, '210 knots at four' and began making a PA." The copilot misinterpreted this as meaning 4,000 feet and started a descent. In this case the captain assumed, justifiably under the circumstances as an inference from *expect*, that the copilot would understand what he meant by " . . . four," because they had both been told to expect " . . . four miles." However, the copilot, having missed that statement, erroneously gave that number what was probably an otherwise more typical interpretation. "Shortly thereafter the controller said to descend to 7,000."[3]

A captain reports reaching 11,000 feet after taking control of the airplane from a confused first officer who had been climbing above an assigned hold-down altitude of 10,000 feet. He suggests "that the reason for the F/O not understanding the clearance was that ATC gave him a heading of 320, EXPECT altitude 230."[4] A controller reports that one aircraft at flight level 220 and another at a higher altitude that was "cleared to descend to FL 230 to anticipate crossing a fix at FL 180" passed each other "with less than 1,000 feet vertical separation." When told that the clearance had been only to FL 230, the pilot of the second plane claimed that he had read back 180, a flight level he had, in fact, only been told to anticipate.[5]

Similarly erroneous inferences may be drawn even when *expect, anticipate,* or their equivalents are not used if the same sort of uncertainty arises in some other way. One might actually spend time trying to answer (75) if one's attention lapses before one reaches the last word, or (76), if one is not familiar with the relevant geography.

(75)   If a plane crashes on the border of the United States and Canada, where do they bury the survivors?

(76)   If a plane crashes on the border of Maine and Massachusetts, where do they bury the victims?

Survivors are not buried, and Maine does not border Massachusetts. In the real incident in (77), *can* is dangerously misconstrued as meaning *do,* with no immediate challenge from the controller.[6]

---

(77)
1. Copilot, cruising at *FL 230,* requests *310.*
2. Controller: *310 is the wrong altitude* for your direction of flight; *I can give you 290* but you will have to negotiate for higher.
3. Copilot: Roger, *cleared to 290, leaving 230.*
4. *No challenge from the controller.*
5. At *24,000 controller* queries altitude and responds: I did not clear you to climb; *descend immediately to FL 230.* You have traffic at eleven o'clock, fifteen or twenty miles.

    Can ⇏ [*Do*]

In effect this is a speech act confusion of the sort discussed in chapter 1, in that the copilot misconstrues a statement of possibility as a giving of permission.

A captain reports having been told twenty miles from his destination "to intercept the localizer and descend to 4,000." Five miles outside the outer marker, level at 4,000 feet, he was told by the Center, "The other aircraft on the approach in front of you has landed; you are number one for the approach," which both the captain and the first officer interpreted as meaning "cleared for the approach." They thus left 4,000 on the glide slope and, two miles outside the marker, at 3,600 feet, they asked the Center for permission to switch to the Tower, to which the Center replied "You were only cleared to 4,000." Another aircraft was departing. The captain explains that even though "the magic words, 'Cleared for the approach'" were never heard (or said), "[we] were under the assumption we were cleared because we were told we were 'number one for the approach' and not told to hold or expect any delay."[7]

Another captain, having been told by the Center that he "would have to be moved to either FL 310 or FL 350" and having been asked by the first officer which he would prefer, replied "flight level 350." Asked his altitude by Center about ten minutes later, he again replied "flight level 350" but was told he had not been cleared to 350." F/O said he had received a clearance and had reported vacating FL 330 for 350." The clearance was mistakenly inferred from the query, and the first officer's report was not noticed.[8]

UNFAMILIAR TERMINOLOGY

Dangerous inferences can also be induced by the use of terminology that is unfamiliar to the addressee. In a particularly striking example, the conversation in (78) is reported to have been overheard.

(78)   Approach Control: We have the REIL [runway end identifier lights] lights up all the way; do you have the runway in sight?
        Pilot (after some hesitation):   How do you tell the difference between real lights and imitation lights?

Because he was unfamiliar with the abbreviation, the pilot inferred a nonexistent distinction.[9]

Another pilot, a flight instructor, asked the Tower "for a transition through their airport traffic," received the reply that he should "circumnavigate the ATA" and inferred that he should therefore remain on his heading and fly through the ATA. "Anticipating a transition through Tower's airspace," he was told instead that he was "in the Airport Traffic Area without a clearance," because, to his surprise, "circumnavigate means remain clear!" Apparently, "one reason controllers use *circumnavigate* (its literal meaning 'to sail around') is to avoid confusion with that other avoidance maneuver, the go-around."[10]

In another instance, a "light airplane was on a right downwind for landing and was instructed by Tower to report base and *sequence behind the special*" that was "on a left downwind for landing." "The civilian pilot asked Tower *if he were clear to land* [and] Tower issued wind, landing clearance, and *instruction to follow the special*," but instead "the light plane . . . turned in front of the special." As a result, "The special pilot initiated a go-around, altered the aircraft to the right, and passed within fifty feet of the civilian aircraft approximately four seconds after initiating the go-around." Upon inquiry the civilian pilot replied that he had not known that he was number two for landing. "The pilot was a student on one of his initial solo flights. He did not clearly understand the instructions given by the Tower."[11]

Another student was "cleared to maintain 1,500 feet after requesting 2,500 feet" and was then "cleared to heading 190 degrees then cleared on course," at which point he "began climb to 2,500 feet." When the instructor reminded him that "he was not cleared out of 1,500 feet," he answered that "he thought [(79)] meant he could climb to requested altitude."[12]

(79)   Cleared on course.

Another pilot was called on altitude when he misinterpreted (80) as meaning that "you are on your own so far as direction and altitude are concerned."

(80)   Resume your own navigation.

In fact, that instruction "does not cancel a previously issued altitude restriction."[13]

A controller reports issuing "an immediate alert—'high terrain at twelve o'clock, three miles, at 4,700 feet,'" upon seeing that an aircraft was descending through 5,000 feet and hearing the MSAW alert. "The aircraft climbed immediately [but] later . . . the flight crew asked . . . for the meaning of" (81).[14]

(81)   low altitude alert

A civilian pilot "confirmed that his aircraft was involved in a near midair" with "two fighter aircraft [that] were in VFR overhead pattern" because he "did not understand the implication when the Tower called his traffic as [(82)], that is, that the fighters would begin a break for downwind at midfield."[15]

(82)   two fighters on initial

Another pilot reports receiving the reply (83) in response to "a request for TCA penetration for a landing at ABC" at fifty miles and then again at twenty-two miles from the TCA boundary.

(83)   Continue.

"My copilot and I discussed the term 'continue' as probably meaning that since the controller didn't own ABC TCA airspace, he would get the approval from ABC on the phone line and then relay the approval to us before entering the TCA's airspace." Repeating the request at seventeen miles, he received the reply (84).

(84)   Contact ABC Approach.

"By this time I was in the TCA and not really sure I had approval or not."[16]

An aircraft passing through 10,000 feet on descent fell too quickly to 8,300 feet and needed to climb back because "the captain, acting as the nonflying pilot, said" (85), "which at that time were new terms to" the copilot.

(85)   ladies, legal, lights, liquids

The captain, a former XYZ airline pilot, explained that these were words the XYZ airline pilots use to remind crew members at 10,000 feet to turn on the seatbelt sign, reduce airspeed to less than 250 knots, turn on the lights for recognition, and make sure the hydraulic pumps and fuel boost pumps are turned on.[17]

Improper terminology can be particularly dangerous when syllables or words of an instruction are omitted. "Some controllers still use such nonstandard phraseologies as [(86)]."

(86)   Cross Warwick not above 6,000 feet.

"Consider the implications if a spike of noise happens to come along and blot out the word *not*."[18]

Air carrier A eastbound at FL 330 had a course crossing with air carrier B southwestbound at 310, but B was seen leaving FL 316 and was stopped "1,000 feet below and 2½ miles away from" A. The controller admits that the main factor in this potential disaster was his having used the improper phraseology (87a), which the pilot misinterpreted as (87b).[19]

(87a)   You might see traffic one o'clock, ten miles, eastbound.
(87b)   Maintain FL 330, traffic one o'clock, ten miles, eastbound.

When a pilot estimated his next checkpoint by stating (88a), the controller wrote (88b) rather than (88c), thereby missing "one little word—'IN'—which would have given a clue about separation."

(88a)   We'll be there in 39.
(88b)   39
(88c)   in 39

The controller explains, "Proper position reporting, nonradar, requires a Zulu clock-time estimate be given. Many pilots do not know that, or want me to do their addition for them."[20]

"After clearing the runway" a crew member "(in the right seat) requested Tower clearance across the active runway to the opposite side of the field" and received what he took to be the reply (89).

(89)   Cleared.

The crew member "glanced to the right, and seeing no aircraft, pilot began to taxi across the runway to the opposite taxiway. Once we were in the middle of the runway, the Tower operator screamed at us . . . to clear the runway. Pilot accelerated the aircraft across the remaining width of the runway, and shortly thereafter a landing light aircraft rolled by." According to the Tower operator, what he had said was (90), but the crew member insists, "The only word the pilot and I heard was [(89)]."

(90)   Remain clear of the runway.

He continues, "This potentially drastic situation could have been avoided if the Tower operator had used standard terminology," such as (91).[21]

(91)   Hold short for landing traffic.

A first officer who received a clearance to cross (92a), instead of the standard (92b), read back (93a), instead of the standard (93b), which would have revealed his error in time to make the crossing, even after getting substantially off course.

(92a)   sixty south at FL 240
(92b)   six zero south at 240

(93a)   sixteen south at 240
(93b)   one six south at 240

When asked to waive the crossing, the controller replied (94), which in practical terms, the reporting crew member points out, "is meaningless."[22]

(94)   Just do the best you can.

An aircraft that had been assigned by the Tower an altitude of 2,000 feet was then told by Departure Control to maintain 4,000 feet and acknowledged. At 2,000 feet, the controller said (95), and the reporting crew member responded (96), meaning "that we were two climbing 4,000," to which the controller replied (97).

(95)   Level 2,000.

(96)   We are two for four.

(97)   Roger.

"At about 2,600 feet the first officer (who was flying) leveled off and pointed out a large air carrier which appeared to be above and in front of us about $\frac{3}{4}$ of a mile," thereby averting a likely disaster. The crew member suggests "the controller may have meant that he wanted us to maintain 2,000 feet when he stated [(95)]," but then he "should have said for us to maintain 2,000 feet, if that is what he wanted us to do. My response could have been more precise, also."[23]

A controller gives the list in (98), "covering just part of my shift, of aircraft that failed to use call signs or used otherwise incorrect phraseology."

---

(98)

1. Air carrier: Issued speed restriction on climbs; answered: "Roger." Four aircraft on frequency at time.
2. Air carrier: Reported on frequency with: "Center, [Flight] with you." He gave no assigned altitude and didn't report out of his present altitude.
3. Air carrier: Inbound, over the fix, issued Approach frequency. No response. We had to check with Approach.
4. Corporate aircraft: Did not use call sign when answering for frequency change.
5. Air carrier: Inbound; no call sign at frequency change.

6. Corporate aircraft: Inbound. Gave descent clearance to maintain seven thousand. Pilot: "Roger; out of nine."
   He did not use call sign, nor did he state assigned altitude.
7. Small GA: Inbound over fix. No call sign on clearance readback (two times); no call sign used at frequency change.
8. Corporate aircraft: No call sign at frequency change.
9. Air carrier: Inbound over fix. No call sign used at frequency change.
10. GA aircraft: Inbound. No call sign used at frequency change.

Examples of Incorrect Phraseology in "a Little More Than an Hour"

He remarks, "Please note that eight of these happened within only thirty-six minutes, all in a little more than an hour!"[24]

And of course not only phrases, but also gestures can be dangerously misunderstood when unfamiliar to the addressee. When a copilot "pointed down and showed four fingers," the pilot took this as confirmation that the aircraft had been cleared to descend to 4,000 feet and so proceeded to leave 9,000, but the copilot had really intended to indicate that the aircraft had been instructed to park via ramp 4 on arrival. The pilot observes, "My copilot is from another country and communicates at times in a different manner."[25]

FALSE ASSUMPTIONS

Error-causing false assumptions can be inferred as a result of distractions, even without linguistic prompts. The incident in (99) was brought about in part by distraction, in that "volume of traffic resulted in an incomplete position briefing" and thus in incomplete knowledge of aircraft position on the part of the responsible controller.[26]

---

(99)
1. Assuming the final position the controller released aircraft B.
2. When B turned downwind aircraft A departed and was immediately in conflict with B.
3. A took evasive action to climb above B, passing over him by 600 feet.

Incomplete Position Briefing Resulting from Volume of Traffic

A pilot reports,

> I was invited to go along with a friend to check out his new airplane. I wanted to fly it around the pattern and as we took

off my door flew open. *I was in the right seat and cleared up the plane as required (lifting gear, etc.).* The other pilot tried to close the door from his side with no luck. He then took the airplane, which he had been checked out in, and told me to try to close the door. The noise was deafening—could not hear the Tower. I heard my friend say "GUMPS," and start the check but I was distracted by the door and continued to try to close it. *I could not see the gear lights and we had no gear horn alarm so I assumed he had put the gear down.* . . . We entered the flare and the props ate the ground. . . . The distraction of the open door and the switch from one PIC to another in midstream caught us off guard. *He did not put the gear down because he did not put it up. I put it up and that didn't register.*[27]

Another pilot reports having been confused in a landing situation while "talking to my passenger, explaining the traffic pattern, about the time I was given the landing instructions," as a result, in part, of "my preconceived ideas about how I would be told to enter the pattern."[28]

A late call-out can induce misleading assumptions about whether a desired flight level has yet been reached. A light aircraft, "outside air 10 degrees at surface, baro 30.16, so climbing like a rocket," flew through its assigned altitude of 12,000 feet to 12,700 feet because the captain, preoccupied with troubleshooting an overheat light, did not call (100) until 11,800 feet.[29]

(100)   1,000 feet before level off

And a pilot reports having incorrectly interpreted a controller's response, (101a), as meaning (101b), after having been "cleared to a heading of 140 degrees and queried if the airport was in sight" and having "verified and . . . requested descent to 2,000 feet" from 3,500.

(101a)   Descend at pilot's discretion.
(101b)   Cleared visually to the airport.

He had earlier been advised that he would be following an airliner, and "the thought that our light twin would catch up to the big jet didn't seem a possibility." He became aware of his error only when he mistakenly began to descend and "could see the airliner on final and realized we were too close to follow."[30]

Mistaken assumptions can also arise from discrepancies between the ways different types of aircraft are treated, as a professional pilot learned when he flew his own plane. Having "asked for VFR advisories westbound" on initial contact, he "was given a squawk and subsequent radar contact [was] established." As he "climbed through 3,000 feet MSL, the departure controller called . . . and stated [(102)], to which he "replied that the TCA was the reason that I was on departure."

(102)   You just violated TCA airspace.

"Immediately another controller came on and said I had to specifically ask for clearance through the TCA," a fact the pilot had not previously been aware of, despite his airline experience. In other words, "being used to operating in the system in one type of aircraft and what to expect from that system does not necessarily apply to the other."[31]

Another pilot, in a similar violation, did not even know that it had occurred. He had "departed VFR and contacted departure," then "told them who I was, where I was, requested 7,500 feet and my intentions" and "was told roger, to squawk * * * * and maintain VFR." Asked at 4,500 feet "to verify altitude (I had mode C)," he replied (103) and then was told "to descend and maintain 3,000 feet," assuming, justifiably, that everything was all right.

(103)   4,500 feet and climbing

The first time he learned that anything inappropriate had occurred was when "three months later I'm notified from the FAA of entering a TCA without authorization."[32]

Yet another source of false assumptions is what one first officer has called "wishful hearing," in which a listener projects what he wants to hear into what is said. His captain had "read back a clearance, including heading and descent, to 10,000 (I thought!)," but the altitude alert sounded at 10,700 feet, and the controller responded to (104) with (105).

(104)   Verify altitude.

(105)   Maintain one one thousand.

"We were in the process of getting updated WX from the second officer [deteriorating] and we were getting close enough that I wanted lower."[33] Another pilot, "stopped at 7,000 due to inbound at 8,000," asked for higher and then misinterpreted the controller's (106) as confirmation of his request.

(106)   Unable; traffic at 8,000.

He apparently missed the words and heard only the number, which is what he was "wishing" for.[34]

An inbound air carrier "was cleared to descend to 12,000 feet," and the Center "missed" the pilot's readback of 10,000 feet. "The aircraft checked in with [Approach Control] out of 16,000 for 10,000," but *"normal altitude for this route is descending to 12,000,"* so this 10,000 was "missed" as well. According to the approach controller who reported the incident, "A minute or so later another aircraft departed [and] when they were about six or seven miles apart, it finally dawned on me that the inbound was level at 10,000 and the outbound was about 9,500 climbing." Their "separation was down to less than the required three miles" before the controller had gotten them onto parallel courses. He adds, "In my opinion the Center controller, the flight crew, and I, the approach controller, all heard what we wanted to hear."[35]

Problems Involving Repetition

KINDS OF REPETITION

Problems of all these sorts, as well as other sorts to be discussed in part 2, are supposed to be—but typically are not—prevented through repetition, which can be categorized along several dimensions.[1] Apparent instances of repetition can be categorized as genuine or virtual, correct or incorrect, full or partial, literal or conceptual, spontaneous or obligatory, and effective or ineffective. A genuine repetition replicates some previous utterance and is intended by the speaker as a replication of that earlier utterance; a virtual repetition resembles some previous utterance in some significant respects but is not intended by the speaker to be such a replication. A correct repetition substantially replicates an earlier utterance in all relevant features; an incorrect repetition fails to replicate some key feature of an earlier utterance that it otherwise matches. A full repetition replicates all of a previous utterance; a partial repetition replicates only part. A literal repetition replicates the words of a previous utterance regardless of the meaning; a conceptual repetition replicates the meaning regardless of the words. A spontaneous repetition arises from a speaker's own initiative based on judgment of a prevailing situation; an obligatory repetition is one a speaker is required to utter by regulation or convention. An effective repetition succeeds in having the impact on the hearer that the speaker intends or that a post hoc observer takes the speaker to have intended or considers that it might have had; an ineffective repetition does not have such an impact.

All these distinctions are clearly evident in the dialogues in (17) and (14). The call sign in line 0133:33 is a virtual repetition, because it looks like a repetition of the call sign in line 0133:11, but in fact it refers to a different aircraft. This contrasts with the call sign in line 1705:53.41, which is a genuine but incorrect repetition of the one in line 1705:44.6. The clearance in the latter line is then repeated literally and correctly in line 1706:09.61, but partially—that is, as (107)—and not conceptually, because it appears to have been misunderstood by the pilot as including a clearance to leave the ground, when the controller seems really to have meant it as a clearance to take effect only after a further clearance to leave the ground is given, as was observed in chapter 1.

(107)   cleared to the Papa Beacon, flight level nine zero, until
           intercepting the three two five

In other words, the words are repeated but not the meaning, at least as intended by the respective speakers. Line 0134:18, in which Air Cal nine thirty one is told to go ahead, is a virtual repetition of line 0134:13, in which Air Cal three thirty six is told to go around. The latter, in turn, contains a genuine repetition of (108), while the former contains an apparent contradiction—that is, conceptual repetition with negation—between *go ahead* and *hold,* which in aviation parlance always means to interrupt what you are now doing and thus, in a landing situation, to go around.

(108)   three thirty six, go around

Since the captain's vernacular use of *hold* in line 0134:16 to mean to continue what he is now doing, and thus to complete his landing, conflicts with this technical usage, the first officer uses the nonliteral conceptual repetition *land* in line 0134:21. The correct, literal, full repetition of the addressee and instruction in line 0134:13 is spontaneous, reflecting the controller's desire to emphasize the urgency of the situation, but it is also ineffective in convincing the pilot actually to go around. The correct, literal, partial repetition of the clearance in line 1706:09.61 is obligatory, reflecting the requirements of the official protocol, and is also effective in convincing the Tower, albeit erroneously, that the clearance has been correctly understood.

This list of distinctions is not intended to be exhaustive but aims simply to provide a useful analytical tool. The distinctions themselves vary in theoretical status and underscore the need to examine both cognitive and social factors in analyzing linguistic data, a fact that is most directly evident in the contrast between spontaneous and obligatory. It also appears that the distinctions are orthogonal—that is, entirely independent—and thus that all possible configurations can occur. For example, it might seem that a nonliteral, nonconceptual repetition, in which neither the words nor the meaning are repeated, would be ruled out, but there could be instances in which the intonation pattern, poetic meter, or rhyme scheme recur, though this is not likely to be of much interest in an aviation setting.

As was just seen for the examples in lines 0134:13 and 1706:09.61, effective and ineffective repetitions are equally capable of undermining the overall success of a longer linguistic interaction, and correct ones are no less capable of doing so than incorrect ones. In the second of these examples, it is the very effectiveness of the repetition, a result of its correctness, that prevents the controller from noticing the pilot's misunderstanding of the intended meaning of the clearance. Confusion between genuine and virtual repetitions can also undermine communicative success, as in the call sign resemblance examples in (17). The full/partial distinction is of special interest in aviation communication and will be examined further in the next section.

FULL AND PARTIAL READBACKS

Special repetitions called full readbacks, in which an entire instruction or a fully synonymous equivalent is repeated in full, play a crucial role in air traffic control through both their presence and their absence. These are required for any instruction a controller issues to a pilot, as a way of confirming that instructions are correctly received and understood.[2] For example, the instruction (109) is supposed to be acknowledged with (110a) or an equivalent, such as (110b).

(109)   Descend to twenty-one thousand feet.

(110a)   Cleared to descend to twenty-one thousand feet.
(110b)   Roger, flight level 210.

However, such requirements are often honored more in the breach than in the observance, as was noted, for example, in

(98). In one three-hour listening session at a major airport, one pilot was recorded responding to the instruction (111a) with (111b), and another responded to a similar instruction with (112), leaving the controller insufficiently informed whether the messages, though received, were understood as intended.[3]

(111a)   Squawk 1735.
(111b)   Squawkin'.

(112)   Awrightee.

Sometimes dangerous near-miss situations arise when partial readbacks rather than full ones occur, as in the actual dialogues in (113) and (114).

---

(113)
1. Controller clears aircraft A to descend to flight level *280*.
2. Controller clears aircraft B to climb to flight level *270*.
3. Controller issues aircraft A a heading of 240.
4. Pilot acknowledges with "Roger two four zero."
5. Aircraft A descends through aircraft B's altitude.
6. Controller observes aircraft A at altitude *27,200* and questions pilot.
7. Pilot claims he was cleared to flight level *240* and he acknowledged it.

Controller: *Heading* ⇒ Pilot: *Flight Level*

---

(114)
1. Aircraft is heading *300* degrees at flight level *270*.
2. Controller gives aircraft a vector to *three one zero*.
3. First officer acknowledges *"three one zero"* but climbs to it instead of turning to it.
4. Captain, temporarily diverted, notices aircraft climbing and corrects error.

Controller: *Vector* ⇒ Pilot: *Flight Level*

Often, "a full readback would eliminate incidents like these." For example, in the first case, "A full readback by the pilot would have prevented the incident as his misunderstanding would have been noticed prior to descending below FL 280."[4]

A readback can sometimes be ineffective because its source has not been made clear. A pilot "requested a climb from FL 280 to 350 and received clearance to climb to 310." While level at 310, he "heard a clearance to climb to 350, read it back, and commenced climb," but at just under 320 the Center called and said (115).

(115)   That clearance wasn't for you; it was for somebody else. Return to 310.

Advised that the clearance had been read back, the controller responded with (116).[5]

(116)   I knew somebody had read back, but I had to see who climbed before I could say anything.

In more complex cases, however, such as the one in (117), even a full readback whose source is known appears not to have been sufficient to remedy the misunderstanding.[6]

---

(117)
1. During climb aircraft is cleared to flight level 310.
2. At about flight level 260 Center controller asks about aircraft's airspeed.
3. Pilot answers "315 knots."
4. Controller replies "Maintain 280."
5. Pilot answers "280 knots," slows to 280 knots, and continues climb to flight level 310.
6. At about flight level 295 controller asks for aircraft's altitude, and pilot replies "295."
7. Controller says aircraft was cleared only to flight level 280.

Controller: *Flight Level* ⇒ Pilot: *Airspeed*

Having established a context of airspeed through his first question and the pilot's fully adequate response, the controller provides insufficient information to indicate that he is changing his topic to flight level. The pilot then gives what amounts to a full readback by combining what the controller actually says ("280") with the already established context ("knots"). In effect, he is reading back the meaning conveyed by the controller's words in context rather than the words themselves, a nonliteral conceptual repetition. Since the controller fails to take notice of the extra word in the pilot's response, a misunderstanding occurs.

And a readback is ineffective even in a simple case when it is not accompanied by an appropriate action by the sender, when it is not heard or is ignored by the addressee, or when the instruction being read back was itself incomplete to begin with. In an instance of the first sort, a pilot reports, "Anticipating 6,000 feet as our assigned altitude, I entered 6,000 in our ALT SELECT. We were subsequently issued a clearance to maintain 5,000." However, "Although I wrote the clearance and read it back verbatim, I inadvertently failed to change the ALT SELECT to 5,000 due to my preoccupation. . . . The wrong entry went unnoticed by both pilots."[7]

In an instance of the second sort, an aircraft that was "cleared to descend to FL 240" was "in the descent and [then] further cleared to cross an intersection at 10,000 feet." The pilot reports, "At approximately 240 the controller gave us traffic at 230 and told him we were descending to 240. I stopped descent at about FL 236 and climbed back up to 240," at which point the dialogue (118) took place.

(118)   Controller: The altitude is 240.
           Pilot: We thought we had been cleared to 10,000.

The pilot observes, "When the copilot responded to the clearance to 10,000 the controller did not indicate disagreement. . . . Perhaps the controller told us to expect ten at the intersection, but when we responded he did not correct us."[8]

In an instance of the third sort, simpler than (117) in that no misleading other context has been set by prior discourse, an aircraft that was "level at FL 230" experienced the dialogue in (119).

(119)   Controller: Maintain 280 (two eight oh).
           Pilot (to first officer):   OK.
           First officer (to controller):   Cleared to maintain 280 (two eight oh).
           [Plane states to climb]
           Controller: Return to 230. That 280 was for airspeed.

The first officer reads back the instruction fully and correctly, after the controller fails to make it clear that the instruction is for airspeed rather than flight level.[9] In a further such example, an aircraft that "had been cleared to 240" and had read that back encountered the wake of their traffic as they descended through FL 250. The Center called as the aircraft "passed through approximately FL 245," but, the pilot notes, "Our descent had just about stopped by the time Center called, as it was apparent to us by then that the traffic was in conflict with our continued descent to FL 240," even though this had been instructed and read back.[10]

REPETITION ACROSS LANGUAGES

A full readback was insufficient to prevent misunderstanding also in the case in (34), in which the controller's wrong choice of verb most likely helped lead the pilot to misconstrue a preposition as a homophonous number. That incident took place "at a foreign airport" where English, though required for aviation communications by international law, is likely otherwise to have been a foreign language. In another incident, a "U.S. military aircraft, on maneuvers in a foreign land, was cleared by the controller" to (120).

(120)   Runway 26 holding position.

The pilot "not inexplicably, understood this to mean" (121) but then found himself facing an aircraft on final that had to take a wave-off.[11]

(121)   Cleared to runway 26; hold in position.

In (122), the pilot tells the copilot, in Spanish, to inform the controller that an emergency prevails, but the copilot tells the controller, in English, only that the plane is running out of fuel.[12]

---

(122)
Pilot to copilot (in Spanish):   Tell them we are in an emergency.
Copilot to controller (in English):   We're running out of fuel.
Pilot to copilot: Digale que estamos en emergencia.
Copilot to pilot: Si, señor, ya le dije.
Copilot to controller (in English):   We'll try once again. We're running out of fuel.
Pilot to copilot (in Spanish):   I don't know what happened with the runway. I didn't see it.
Copilot to pilot (in Spanish):   I didn't see it.
Pilot to copilot (in Spanish):   [Advise the controller that] we don't have fuel.
Copilot to controller (in English):   Climb and maintain 3,000 and, ah, we're running out of fuel, sir.
Controller to copilot (in English):   Is that fine with you and your fuel?

Copilot to controller (in English):   *I guess so.* Thank you very much.
[Aircraft runs out of fuel and crashes]

Cove Neck, New York, 25 January 1990

He then tells the pilot, in Spanish, that he has conveyed that
the plane is in an emergency, even though that is not, in English, what he has actually said. The controller utters what he
erroneously takes to be, three conceptual repetitions of the
pilot's words—that is, (123a) for (123b).[13]

(123a)   running out of fuel
(123b)   in an emergency

These are ineffective in conveying to the controller the proper
degree of urgency, because the heightened sense of urgency
conveyed by *emergency* in the aviation context makes the repetitions incorrect. The problem is probably compounded here,
as in (34), by the fact that the language being used is a technical
variant of a language other than the speaker's own, leaving
him twice removed from the vernacular with which he is most
familiar. The aircraft subsequently ran out of fuel, and 73 of the
159 people aboard died in the resulting crash, including the
three crew members in the cockpit.

   Language conflict may also have been operative in (35),
which resembles the near miss in (34). In that accident, which
occurred at "a Southeast Asian airport—in marginal visual
conditions at night," "an experienced U.S. freighter crew" erroneously, though quite justifiably, gave what they took to be a
full readback, but "there was no correction of this readback by
the Tower." In consequence, "About eight miles short of the
runway the aircraft struck the ground. All aboard were killed."

COGNIZANCE, ENGAGEMENT, AND RITUALIZATION

The requirement to give full readbacks, like other official constraints on language use, can be expected to be successful in
preventing miscommunication only when both interlocutors
are fully cognizant of the subtle nuances of the language they
are using and fully engaged in their role as interlocutors.
Speakers of languages in which explicit prepositions figure
less prominently than they do in English may be more likely to

omit such words, if the danger of doing so is not brought specifically to their attention in training. In both (117) and (54), the
controller could have prevented the respective incidents by
simply noticing that the readback did not match what he had
said (or meant).

As was seen in chapter 1, the confusions and cross-purposes
involved in (17) resulted, despite several repetitions of words
or meanings, in Air California 336's landing with its gear
retracted, having finally decided to go around, but too late
actually to do so, and the misconstrued clearance in (14) led to
collision with another aircraft that was still on the runway. The
captain's noncompliance in the former instance and the incorrect call sign repetition in the latter suggest degrees of engagement that were, for whatever reason, less than adequate.

In the incident in (54), as was observed in chapter 2, though
the crew members repeat at least three times[14] that they are
unable to get their nose-gear light to go on, the controller asks
(124), using *things* in reference to a decline in elevation that he,
but not the crew, has noticed on radar.[15]

(124)   how are things comin' along

He fails to realize that the special salience of the nose-gear
problem for the crew, as indicated by all those repetitions, and
the lack of salience for them of elevation, since he has not mentioned it explicitly, will prevent them from understanding that
reference. The crew members, in turn, reinforce their own preoccupation with the nose-gear light through their repeated references to it, while failing to realize that, as a result of various
hand-offs, those repetitions are addressed to different interlocutors who do not individually experience these repetitions
and are therefore not so reinforced.

It may be that the routine nature of much aviation communication, and of repetition in particular, induces a degree of ritu-
alization, with statements and situations losing their cognitive
impact and participants falling into a pattern of simply going
through the motions for their own sake.[16] For example, an aircraft that had been "cleared to 16,000" descended to 15,600 feet
before its descent was stopped, because "every altitude from
takeoff through descent was [of the form (125)]."

(125)   Cleared to –– feet; expedite.

"Consequently, on descent through 18,000, resetting altimeters, altitude alert missed at 17,000 feet. Flight engineer was also distracted talking on company frequency. 'The perfect set-up.' "[17]

A pilot relates, "Just after the 'three mile final' report we took evasive action to avoid a small aircraft that had been instructed to follow us. He had acknowledged and reported us in sight." The pilot explains, "I believe he saw another aircraft and ASSUMED we had misrepresented our position."[18] Following the dialogue in (126), a pilot reports, "we started our turn and (thinking we had been cleared for a visual approach) began a descent," but were then told by the controller that "he had not yet cleared us below 4,000."[19]

(126)   Controller: Can you see the runway?
         Pilot: Yes.
         Controller: Okay, turn to 360 degrees.

In both cases, the very familiarity of the landing process misled the pilots into hearing more or assuming other than what was actually said.

In another incident, an instructor pilot and his student "in a block altitude of 12,000–14,000 feet . . . both thought the controller told them to turn left to a heading of 010 degrees and descend to and maintain 10,000 feet," but when they reached 10,700 "the controller stated the aircraft had been cleared to 12,000 not 10,000." The instructor explains: "There are two contributing causes for this occurrence: 99 percent of all clearances from that area are to descend and maintain 10,000, and as the instructor I was conditioned to descend to 10,000 by many previous flights. The controller may have said 12,000 but I was programmed for 10,000."[20]

The final example of "wishful hearing" at the end of chapter 3 also seems to fit this pattern. Such occurrences suggest that the standardization of terminology and protocol, though necessary up to a point, may be counterproductive beyond that point, and that ways will therefore have to be found to maintain meaningful interest among participants in the air-ground communication process. With a semiautomated communication system of one of the sorts discussed in part 3, a random number generator could be used to select, unpredictably, from among a set of standard formulations for a desired instruction, thereby preventing the constant, boredom-inducing repetition of the same formulation. In the unlikely event that one formulation does get selected many times in succession, that very occurrence, in that setting, would itself be cause for surprise and therefore perk up attention.

Part II

Communication Problems
Not Based on Language

Problems with Numbers

NUMBERS

Though commonly thought to be inherently more precise and accurate than other aspects of language, the use of numbers—the aspect that most directly interfaces with technical equipment—is in fact a prolific source of misunderstanding, such as when "ABC airline designates extra sections of popular flights as ABC flight 123B, 123C, etc." or when "Dogpatch eight and Air Dogpatch eighty-eight [are] on the same frequency, being worked by the same controller, within a few miles of one another."[1] One pilot observes: "It is patently ridiculous to have our sky filled with flights calling themselves ex-zero-something-something when the something-something alone would suffice. . . . Our [airline's] action in bailing out of the X000-series call sign group did much to ameliorate the situation and it would be equally easy and effective for the biggest of several commuters serving any one hub to do likewise."[2] In other such examples, "runway two zero is sometimes confused with runway two," or "flight 925 takes a clearance intended for flight 529" in an addressee confusion of the sort discussed in chapter 2.[3] Or "'one six thousand' is read back as 'six thousand' [and the] controller fails to notice error. . . . 'Five' and 'nine' are conspicuous gotchas" as a result of their near homophony, of the sort examined in chapter 1.[4]

A pilot reports being in "a descent from 8,000 feet when we heard one and possibly two flights on approach with our flight number, one of which answered a call for us or the other flight with our number." The first officer tried to call and verify the assigned altitude, but "due to radio traffic from the other flights with our number . . . he was unable to call for about a minute." Upon inquiry "the controller said we should be at

8,000 feet and we began a climb from approximately 5,600 feet back to 8,000 feet."[5] As another pilot observes, "We must develop a more emphatic/no confusion (foolproof!) call sign system where aircraft of similar call signs are in the same airspace—especially on the same 'Alpha 1234 RED' . . . in order to lessen the confusion over who should respond."[6] Similar flight numbers led aircraft A to mistake aircraft B's clearance to take off from runway 10 as a clearance for itself to take off from runway 19. According to aircraft B, "Because of our configuration and speed we could continue only straight ahead. We passed about 1,000 feet behind him."[7]

An international carrier inbound to the United States was handed off to a new Center after the captain read back the clearance (127a) and the first officer set the altitude selector to 20,000; to the initial contact from the flight (127b) the Center responded (127c).

(127a)   Cleared *to* descend to two zero *zero,* cross *two zero* miles
          south of XYZ at two two zero.
(127b)   Leaving two two zero for *two zero zero.*
(127c)   Were you cleared to two zero *zero?*

The Center claimed later that the clearance had been only to 220, but the crew understood otherwise. They pointed out that the word *maintain* had not been used and that at the time of the query a new clearance could have been issued to maintain 220.[8]

Another frequent problem with numbers involves "mistaking clearances to 'one zero thousand' and 'one one thousand' feet. There is enough similarity between the words to cause consistent confusion [and] the problem is enhanced due to one zero thousand being a transition altitude."[9] A first officer "set the altitude alert to 10,000 feet," in response to the clearance (128), and according to the captain, "It wasn't until ATC questioned our altitude that we realized that we were not where we were supposed to be."[10]

(128)   Descend to *one one thousand ten miles* north of the city at
         250 knots.

A pilot who responded to the clearance (129a) with (129b) reached 10,500 feet before Approach Control radioed (129c).[11]

(129a)   At the forty DME descend to *one one thousand* feet.
(129b)   Roger at the forty DME descend to *one zero thousand* feet.
(129c)   Climb immediately to *one one thousand* feet.

And in the incident in (130) such a confusion almost leads to a midair collision.[12]

---

(130)
1. Controller: ABC where are you going? Your assigned altitude was *one zero thousand!*
2. ABC pilot: XYZ Approach, we understood our clearance was to *one one thousand;* we read back *one one thousand.* . . .
3. Controller: Negative, ABC! Turn right to zero nine zero degrees and descend immediately to *one zero thousand.* You have traffic at *one one thousand,* twelve o'clock –– miles.

Ten Thousand ⇒ *Eleven Thousand*

A possible solution to this problem might be to adopt the policy "that one zero thousand be called over the radio as 'ten' thousand and leave eleven thousand as 'one one thousand.' This would differentiate the levels enough so that [such] repeated clearances, mistaken altitudes, and potential near misses could be averted."[13]

Sometimes hearing too many numbers at once can confuse a listener as to which number is which. An "air carrier, at 16,000, had a descent clearance to 12,000 because of crossing traffic, a small aircraft. The air carrier had not started his descent." The reporting controller "told him to start his descent about fifteen miles northeast of the fix and to plan on crossing thirty miles north of the airport at or below 9,000 to maintain 6,000." The pilot then "read back the clearance and said [(131)]."

(131)   Starting down now.

The controller "called traffic to the small aircraft when the two aircraft got a little closer and was about to call traffic to the air carrier," but then "observed his altitude 1,500 feet below 12,000" and so "questioned his altitude." The pilot responded that "he thought his clearance was to 6,000," so the controller advised him "that clearance was to 12,000" and that that was what the controller had "thought he understood." The controller observes, "Pilot should have read back altitude starting down to –– and I should have reiterated [(132)]."[14]

(132)   Roger, descending to (altitude).

Digits can also be reversed. A departing pilot who had been assigned (133a) read back without challenge a new clearance to (133b) but was then told when he reached 150 degrees "that the correct heading had really been 210."[15]

(133a)   heading 225 degrees, climb to 5,000
(133b)   FL 230, heading 120 degrees

Sometimes such a reversal can distract attention from an even more serious error. Inbound flight *XY*, "cleared to cross an intersection at the Approach Control boundary at or below 15,000, to maintain *12,000*," read back (134).

(134)   Roger, airline *YX* . . . is cleared to cross at or below 15 for *10*.

The controller noticed that the pilot had transposed the digits in the call sign but failed to notice that he had read back the wrong altitude. "Subsequently the aircraft, at 10,000 feet, passed within about two miles of an opposite direction air carrier climbing out."[16] The Tower cleared a military trainer for an "unrestricted climb to FL 310," after TRACON had approved an altitude of only 13,000 feet. Subsequent investigation revealed that the flight's initial clearance had included (135), a problematic *expect* instruction of the sort discussed in chapter 3 (Lexical Inference).

(135)   Expect FL 310 after crossing 235 radial.

The pilot's readback was correct except for his departure frequency, which he read back as "318.4" rather than "381.4." After takeoff Departure Control was unable to reach him at 381.4 and so "notified Center that the flight was a no radio."[17]

Readbacks can also be ineffective in correcting number confusions. In response to the clearance (136a), a pilot can hear (136b) and read back (136c), in response to which the controller hears (136d) and states (136e).[18]

(136a)   Turn left heading 210.
(136b)   310
(136c)   Turn left heading 310.
(136d)   210
(136e)   Clearance correct.

On the controller's part, this may be a form of "wishful hearing," as discussed in chapter 3, since he already knows what
he has told the pilot and thus what response he wants to hear.
While a "flight attendant was passing a meal tray over the
flight engineer to the captain," a captain "received clearance to
descend from FL 330 to FL 190 and acknowledged according to
standard procedure." The Center later told him that the clearance had really been to FL 290, but only while he was passing
FL 270.[19] A first officer "set 17,000 in the altitude select window" after the captain "acknowledged a 7,000 feet restriction."
The captain reports, "Center called, wanted to know where we
were going," but not until "we passed 12,000."[20]

In an incident that "reflected a fairly rare double hearback
failure," a small transport checked in as (137a) but was thought
by the reporting controller to be saying (137b), leading to "minimum separation" between that aircraft and a "departure coming out at 7,000."

(137a)   descending to 6,000 feet
(137b)   descending to 8,000

It turned out upon investigation that the "center had cleared
the aircraft to eight before handing it off to Approach. The
tapes showed that the readback was to six to both controllers
and went unnoticed both times."[21]

Sometimes controllers fail to catch a pilot's numerical mistakes, as in the last few examples, or as when a pilot "mistakenly copied the altimeter setting as 30.59" from "the ATIS
information" and then "read back the setting given by the
controller," who "in the busy state of affairs . . . missed [the
pilot's] error." The aircraft "leveled at what we thought was
11,000 feet," because "the controller didn't advise us that we
were at 10,000." After being "given clearance to 3,500 feet we
descended and leveled off there," at which point "the controller told us that we were at 2,500 feet. We climbed back up to
3,500 after resetting our altimeter."[22]

Another pilot thought he had "received descent clearance to
cross the VOR at 240. During the descent [he was] advised of
traffic at twelve o'clock low," which turned out to be "at the
same altitude." According to the pilot, "The captain told me to
pull up just as the Center called to ask us to verify our altitude." The controller stated that he had cleared the aircraft to

250, but the pilot claimed to have been "certain that he cleared us to 240."[23]

At other times it is a controller who saves the day, as when "all altimeters were in error," because "the cross-check of altimeters was only that they agreed—not the barometric input," *the stand-by altimeter with the correct ATIS value of 29.36 having been reset to 30.36 to agree with the incorrect value shown on the captain's and first officer's altimeters.* An "alert controller corrected the error before it was a critical problem" by noticing an altitude discrepancy and then asking for altimeter verification.[24] In another incident, a pilot who had been asked "to report leaving 4,000 and reaching 5,000 . . . reported leaving 4,000" and then reported that "he was leaving 4,800." At this point the controller noticed that "his mode C readout showed 3,800 [and] so . . . informed him of this and asked him to verify altitude." Although the pilot thought he was "level at 5,000," the controller "realized that he was 1,000 feet low—actually at 4,000—and head-on to traffic." The pilot had been given an altimeter setting of 29.43 but had set it to 30.43 instead; "fortunately the controller was able to descend the aircraft (which should have been a safe thousand feet above his traffic) and avert a close call."[25]

RANGE OVERLAPS

Perhaps the most pervasive numerical confusions are those that arise because of the overlapping number ranges that are used for the various flight parameters. In (113), (114), and (117), for example, a heading, a vector, and an airspeed, respectively, are confused with a flight level, as was observed in chapter 4 (Full and Partial Readbacks). A pilot reports, "On climb out, approaching our cleared altitude of 14,000 feet the captain took and read back a clearance to turn to *heading two eight zero.* The copilot, flying, thinking the clearance was to climb to *flight level two eight zero,* started a climb."[26] A pilot with a single-engine VFR in traffic pattern reports the two incidents in (138), which occurred within a space of two weeks.[27]

---

(138)	Incident 1

1. Tower: Make a three-sixty for better traffic separation.
2. Pilot: You mean make another circle of the airport?
3. Tower: Negative. Make a three-sixty in place.

Incident 2

[Two weeks later, same pattern, different airport]

1. Tower: Make a three-sixty for better traffic separation.
2. Pilot: You mean in place?
3. Tower: Negative. Make another circuit of the field.

---

360 ≠ 360

In (139) a 360 heading to follow a river is misunderstood as a 360 turn to follow traffic.[28]

---

(139)

1. Approach control: *Left 360, descend to 3,000, follow river.*
2. Copilot: Understand a *left 360* and *descent to 3,000?*
3. Approach: Firm; *following traffic* ten o'clock, six miles.
4. Copilot: Roger; looking for the traffic and we're doing a *left 360 to follow.*
5. Approach (halfway around):   What are you doing?
6. Copilot: *A left 360 to follow traffic* as instructed!
7. Approach: Climb to 4,000 now; role out heading 360 for vectors to follow traffic.

Heading ⇒ Turn

Asked to confirm a "previously assigned altitude as 9,000 feet," a pilot replied (140) and then noted his heading as 110.

(140)   Negative, assigned one one thousand.

He "questioned the first officer if [the] heading was supposed to be 090" and "then realized that we may have confused the heading and altitude assignment (90 degrees and 11,000 for 9,000 and one one zero degrees)."[29]

A pilot reports having interpreted (141) as an altitude restriction, 11,000 feet, when it was intended by a controller as a time restriction, eleven zulu.[30]

(141)   Cross the intersection at eleven.

In the incident in (142), a speed reduction clearance was misinterpreted as a flight level clearance, because the Center deleted the word *knots* after the initial speed reduction request to 270.[31]

---

(142)

1. Aircraft at *flight level 370* receives clearance to *descend to flight level 330.*

2. Aircraft receives clearance understood as *descend to 270.*
3. Aircraft reads back *"leaving 330 for 270."*
4. Aircraft begins descent. At *flight level 325* Center requests altitude, which aircraft reports as *32,500.*
5. Center requests that aircraft return to *flight level 330* and aircraft immediately complies. Aircraft is then requested to *slow to 270.*

Speed ⇒ Flight Level

Another flight crew misinterpreted a speed of 210 knots as a heading of 210 degrees because "the controller intending to give the speed restriction rose from his chair to coordinate with his adjacent mate, lost his balance, and hit the neighboring controller on the head with his telephone." He was thus unable to clarify his intended meaning.[32]

A captain reports step climbing toward cruise altitude, "with stops at FL 290, 310, and 330." After a few minutes level at 330, "Center called with a transmission that included the numbers '350' and the first officer read back" the reply (143). "I didn't hear the full transmission."

(143)   Climb to 350.

Shortly after climbing to and leveling off at FL 350, they were told by Center that the 350 had really been a heading.[33] A pilot reports being leveled by Center at FL 280 and then being told by the controller that "he would have higher when we were clear of traffic." Being distracted, the pilot did not hear the copilot say (144) but did hear the controller say (145).

(144)   We are still on a 295 degree heading.

(145)   Make it 290.

"He did not say degrees, heading, speed, or anything—just '290.'" Being in a step-climb mode, the pilot interpreted the number as an altitude, "turned the altitude reminder to 290 and started to climb." At FL 285 he checked with the copilot, who called to confirm and was told by the controller that the 290 was a heading.[34] Another pilot, while descending on a standard arrival, responded to what he thought was (146a) with (146b).

(146a)   Turn to 270 degrees and slow to 250 knots.
(146b)   Turn to due west and down to two five zero.

While passing through FL 270, "we heard someone else at FL 260 and immediately questioned the controller," who told them that the 270 had been intended as a flight level. "The aircraft had descended to 26,000 and was immediately returned to FL 270. No evasive action was necessary."[35]

An aircraft passed a fix and then "departed it on the 273 degree radial instead of the 320 degree magnetic heading," having "mistaken one VOR for another."[36] In another incident, an "air carrier cleared via heading 180 degrees to intercept 034 degree radial . . . turned northeast on radial in face of another aircraft at the same altitude. I had to descend that aircraft immediately without coordination," the controller reports, "due to fact that first aircraft was no longer on my frequency." The "pilot later explained that he confused [(147)] with [(148)]."[37]

(147)   radial 034

(148)   heading 034

In what is perhaps the most strikingly perverse and thought-provoking example of what can reasonably be interpreted as a range conflict, though of a somewhat different nature from those discussed here thus far, "a westbound aircraft at flight level 390 . . . was cleared in error to descend through FL 350." This altitude "happened to be occupied at the time by another aircraft approaching head-on and not so far away," but "by chance, the two were on opposite sides of the International Date Line." Technically, "it was Friday for one of the aircraft and Saturday for the other," so they were separated numerically by more than the standard twenty-four hours and thus were not in conflict![38] Again, a semiautomated communication system of one of the sorts described in part 3 could be specifically programmed to look out for such anomalies.

ALTIMETERS

The use of altimeters is a particularly prolific source of wrong numbers, as has already been seen in the last few examples of the preceding section on numbers, and therefore deserves special attention: "A recent issue of the excellent naval air safety publication *Approach* carried a tale about a navy transport which, commencing an ILS approach at a European airport was given QNH 992. The flight crew had become accustomed to the European controllers' policy of providing

USA crews with altimeter settings in inches of mercury, so interpreted this as 29.92."[39] Another crew thought they were at 2,000 feet until the controller told them that they were at 1,500 and that the altimeter was (149).

(149)   QNH nine nine two.

"Almost instinctively, we inserted 992 millibars into the copilot's altimeter . . . and the actual altitude displayed was 1,450 feel MSL—a difference of 550 feet."[40] The lead of a flight of two fighters was cleared by the Center out of cruising altitude with the clearance (150), acknowledged, and then set his altimeter to 30.34.

(150)   Maintain 5,000, altimeter 29.34.

Neither lead nor wing cross-checked instruments until the Center reported they were 500 feet low and recleared them to 4,000 feet.[41] Another aircraft flew 400 feet low because the altimeter had been set to 30.20 instead of the correct value of 29.84. "The first officer had mistakenly read . . . the transponder squawk instead of the current altimeter setting, which was written on the same note pad."[42]

Sometimes a crew will hear only part of such a number and so will guess what the rest of it was, thereby risking the introduction of false assumptions of the sort discussed in chapter 3. When an aircraft was found to be "nearly 1,000 feet low," it turned out that the flight crew had "heard only [the] last two digits of [the] altimeter setting [and so] took a chance on 30.45."[43] In another incident, "The altimeters were set to 30.41" instead of 29.41 because "the ATIS was fuzzy but .41 came through."[44] Sometimes, as in these examples and in the one in (151), the missing digits are simply not heard.[45]

---

(151)
1. Center: Aircraft B, descend at pilot's discretion to maintain one six thousand. Altimeter XXXX.
2. Aircraft B: Roger, aircraft B cleared to six thousand.
3. Aircraft B (shortly thereafter):   B is leaving 430 for six thousand.
4. Center: Roger.
5. Aircraft A: Center, this is A. Just out of curiosity, we thought we heard you clear the other aircraft to one six thousand and he read back six thousand twice and you acknowledged. Which is correct?

6. Center: <u>One</u> *six thousand!* Aircraft B, *maintain sixteen thousand;* that's <u>one six</u> *thousand.*
7. Aircraft <u>B</u>: B, descending to *one six thousand.* We were just about to ask you about that.

Controller: *16,000* ⇒ Pilot: *6,000*

Other times they are omitted deliberately, as when a pilot was told (152) by the Center.

(152)   Altimeter, nine, eight, six.

He warns, "If it becomes commonplace to abbreviate altimeter settings" in this way, then "one day the abbreviated setting will be transmitted to a foreign carrier who will set in 986 millibars instead of 29.86." He notes that it has already become "commonplace . . . to abbreviate radio frequencies by deleting the first digit (e.g., 121.9 becomes 'twenty-one nine')."[46]
    Altimeter errors occur for many reasons. There can be a discrepancy between the Center and Approach Control, as when a crew was told by the latter "they showed us at 9000+," even though the crew members thought they "had not yet reached 10,000" in their descent. "Approach gave us altimeter setting 29.66, not 30.66 which we both thought—and still believe—was given us by Center and which I had written down along with the clearance."[47] There can be old information that has not been updated, as when an aircraft found on landing, "during a big storm in the area," that "at field elevation the altimeter read 110 feet high." They had "received ATIS information . . . nearly one hour old," with an altimeter setting of 30.08, when they had been "about 125 miles out." By the time they were "handed off to Approach, . . . the ATIS had evidently been changed," with a new altimeter setting of 29.97, "but we were not told of this. We were also not given a new altimeter setting, nor did we request one." Furthermore, "Tower had not given us an updated altimeter either; we never requested it as we were preoccupied with turbulent approach."[48] A number can be in error simply because another number has been misread, as when a pilot, after takeoff, "called Departure Control and reported out of 1,200 for 10,000," rather than out of the correct value of 2,200, an error "the controller did not catch." When

the "aircraft came from the hangar after an engine change with the altimeters reading 28.89," the copilot and pilot mistakenly read them as 29.89, "as given on the ATIS."[49] Automated cross-checking of communications could go a long way toward preventing or correcting all these sorts of errors.

Problems with Radios

No Radio

Just as great a source of miscommunication as the use of altimeters is the use and misuse of radios and, in particular, having no radio. A pilot reports "complete electrical failure" as "darkness was rapidly setting in" and the consequent need to communicate with the Tower by "blinking a flashlight."[1] Another pilot who "had flown to the airport . . . on an IFR clearance . . . had neglected to change the squawk code to VFR upon cancellation of IFR clearance." He "overlooked the transponder code setting" and "flew to the VORTAC without noticing the incident," because he "was unable to hear the Center due to poor radio reception."[2]

A captain reports losing communication with the Center "for one to two minutes" when "the earpiece for my headset disconnected from the headset" while "the first officer was trying to get the ATIS" and thus "was off the ATC frequency." The disconnection was discovered only when "passengers . . . hooked up to the ATC channel of the audio entertainment system . . . heard Center trying to call us [and] reported this to the flight attendants who, in turn, came to the cockpit to check on us."[3] A pilot "turned the volume down on the VOR radio [and] evidently turned the volume down on the VHF next to it" unintentionally at the same time. It was only after "not hearing anything on Center frequency for some time" and hearing no side tone when he called the Center that he realized that "the volume control was turned all the way down." Turning it up and calling the Center again, he "was informed that they had been trying to contact us for eighty miles. We had to do a 360 degree turn so we could be handed off to Approach control."[4]

Just as missing part of a number can lead to risky number guessing, as was observed in chapter 5, not having a radio can also lead to dangerous false assumptions of the sort discussed in chapter 3. The incident in (153) took place at a non-Tower airport with a flight service station (FSS).

---

(153)
1. Aircraft C is on six mile final for runway 27.
2. Aircraft A is told by Flight Service that runway 18 is in use.
3. Aircraft A advises that he will use runway 36.
4. Aircraft A is again told that 18 is favored.
5. Aircraft C lands and rolls across the intersection.
6. Aircraft A announces that if C will hold his position, A will depart.
7. Aircraft B, *with no radio,* now taxies into takeoff position on 18.
8. Both Aircraft A and B initiate takeoff roll at the same time.
9. Aircraft A rotates south of the intersection. Aircraft B abruptly stops his takeoff roll, thereby averting a head-on collision.

No Radio ⇒ False Assumption

Runways 9/27 and 18/36 intersect at their midpoints, and winds were light. Immediately following the near collision, "Because of A departing on 36, the pilot of NORDO aircraft B *assumed* that the runway was in use, and taxied to runway 36 for departure." The reporting flight service specialist continues, "The whole scenario was about to be repeated with aircraft D, who was departing runway 18. Luckily, aircraft B's pilot spotted the traffic!"[5]

Equally dangerous is the problem of having too few radios. During VFR operation a pilot was cleared by the approach controller "to land without instructions to contact or monitor Tower frequency." After touchdown he did monitor the Tower frequency and was finally reached by the Tower during rollout. Inquiring why a switch to the Tower was not given, he was advised that he should have contacted the Tower without instruction. "This would not have been a problem with two radios. If pilot had only one, contacting Tower without instruction would have required leaving assigned frequency."[6]

Nonuse or Misuse of Radio

More disturbing are incidents in which an available radio is simply not used. One aircraft landed without clearance because "the captain simply forgot to contact Tower."[7] A pilot reports that after just landing, he "perceived a BIG twin, with landing lights aglow, on final for landing on 25. No radio transmission had been undertaken by this twin, and none was heard as he landed."[8] Another pilot reports being told on takeoff "to hold our position and cancel takeoff clearance," after his aircraft had been rolling about two hundred feet. "Still in position, next thing we knew aircraft came right over the top of us, missing us—it seemed like by inches. His thrust rocked our aircraft as he initiated a go-around," coming within five feet of touching down. It turned out that "he was never on Tower frequency . . . and never heard the go-around call."[9]

A pilot reports being "unable to receive acknowledgment from Center after several attempts. Turned transponder off to determine radio condition. Controller at this time acknowledged and requested transponder be turned on."[10] Another pilot initiated an immediate go-around when he sighted an aircraft in takeoff position, discovering only later "that Tower had been advising us to go around. . . . It never occurred to them that perhaps I wasn't receiving their transmissions."[11] An aircraft landing on runway 23 had to go around suddenly because of "a small plane getting much larger just touching down on other end of 23 (runway 5)," and it thereby "evaded the oncoming aircraft by about fifty to seventy-five feet vertical and one hundred feet horizontal. . . . At no time did the other aircraft call prior to approach, nor did he ask for advisory." It turned out that that aircraft's pilot "was an instructor filling out his student's logbook. His comment: 'Well, we used 5 for takeoff.'"[12]

Sometimes not using the radio is entirely accidental, as when a pilot "just flat forgot to contact Tower" during a landing[13] or when another forgot to turn up the volume. As the latter pilot's crewmate explains: "Usually the volume control on the radio is set according to the level of cockpit noise. Which means that when you forget to turn up the volume you don't hear the controller say, 'cancel takeoff clearance; hold in position.' Unless you're wearing those little foam earplugs—which I was. Other pilot (at the controls) without earplugs and having forgotten his headset never heard the controller."[14] Another pilot thought he had been cleared to cross a runway—"As if I could hear the controller say it in my head"—but then as he approached the runway, he "switched the radio to Tower frequency and at this time . . . noticed the volume control on the radio turned full down."[15]

Sometimes the radio cannot be used because someone else has inadvertently blocked it off. A controller reports that on "a busy weekend" with "good weather with full traffic patterns at controlled and uncontrolled airports," an "airline pilot calls several times to contact a friend at a UNICOM too far away to hear," commenting that "he was '. . . at FL 270, just passing through.'" "During the couple of minutes of irrelevant conversation, who knows how many traffic patterns were blocked out by the airliner's fifty-watt transmitter?"[16] "When you key your microphone you block off your receiver on that frequency—right? Partly right. *You also block out every other receiver tuned to that frequency in the area.* Inadvertent keying of the transmitter is a growing problem that can create danger for any pilot in the air traffic system."[17] In fact, exactly this happened when a "stuck mike" cut off all communications for a brief period during a three-hour listening session at a major airport.[18] In a similar incident, a pilot who had "contacted Approach on the assigned frequency as well as the previously assigned frequency to no avail . . . then noticed the transmit light was steady 'on,' on both radios." Upon further checking, he found that "due to the severe turbulence . . . that day, the hand-held mike had jumped out of its holder and was wedged between the seats with the button on."[19] "Recurring stuck mike problems reported by an ATC facility" prompted NASA's Aviation Safety Reporting System to issue an alert in late 1992.[20]

In another instance, a pilot "finally taxied to the active runway and contacted Tower, having never gotten through to Ground," because "Ground Control frequency was totally clogged with numerous aircraft trying to call at once." The "controller's response to the jammed frequency was to broadcast repeatedly, 'one aircraft call at a time,' which led to several seconds of silence and then everybody calling at once."[21] Another time, "a pilot climbing through FL 260 was sure he had been cleared to the requested 370, but some little question in his mind caused him to ask Center for confirmation." Instead, he received in reply "a resounding" (154).

(154)   NEGATIVE! Maintain 260.

"He was quite certain of what he had heard, but there were other transmissions on the air and he suspects possible interference or blockage of part of the clearance he believed was for him."[22] In a separate instance, another pilot "waited for a break in the heavy volume of radio traffic to get in a call," while "several calls were cut out by people transmitting over each other." When he did manage to get through, he reports, "I was directly north of the field but mistakenly called my position as [(155a)]. Evidently all they heard was [(155b)]."

(155a)   north and east
(155b)   east

He suggests, "So much confusion could be avoided if everybody would use common radio courtesy and listen before transmitting."[23]

And sometimes not using the radio is actually a matter of policy. A helicopter "was inbound to the airport in straight and level flight when a small airplane was first sighted by our crew chief . . . in a diving turn coming directly at us (within fifty to seventy-five feet) when first spotted." Even after immediate evasive action was taken to avoid a midair collision, "the proximity of the two aircraft at closest converging point was ten to fifteen feet." After landing, the helicopter pilot was told by the other pilot that "he had seen us and the pass was intentional" with the objective "to show his passenger the helicopter. The pilot was charging for rides to view the fall foliage." Throughout the incident "there was no radio contact between the two aircraft." Before the incident the airport manager had advised the helicopter crew "that radio communication should be kept to a minimum." After the incident the manager advised them "that *radios in many aircraft were not turned on, to save wear and tear on equipment.*"[24]

Refusing to use the radio can complicate already dangerous situations. The entire incident in (156) took place "in the span of eighteen minutes," with runway 10 in use.

(156)

1. Two light aircraft in pattern for 10, both monitoring 123.6 AAS frequency. FSS has an IFR inbound on a four-engine military plane, Center estimate :30.
2. At :28 a light aircraft lands on 10.
3. Seconds later the military aircraft rumbles onto runway 22, out of nowhere, unannounced (*no radio contact*).
4. The light aircraft has to expedite landing rollout and turnoff in order to avoid the larger military aircraft at the runway intersection.
5. The military plane taxies into ramp, parks in front of FSS, and pilot looks eyeball to eyeball with FSS for ten minutes while disembarking passenger.
6. *Despite FSS gestures to get the military pilot to use the radio, he does not get the message.*
7. Military plane begins taxiing for 10, holds short of runway for run-up, and watches the next sequence develop (*still no radio contact with FSS*).
8. Two light aircraft A and B are in pattern. A reports base for 10 at :40.
9. At :41, A reports final for 10, B reports base for 10, and C (another light aircraft—*previously unannounced*) cuts in front of A and B, reports short final for 10, and asks for airport advisory.
10. C makes a slow, deliberate landing on 10. A, only about one hundred feet behind C, lands also. B, noticing it is getting rather crowded, announces he will make a go-around.
11. C, who landed first, putters along on rollout, finally turns off on taxiway just as A zips by. They miss each other by about twenty feet.
12. Military aircraft begins moving on 10, apparently on takeoff roll (*still no radio contact*), then slows down and decides to taxi down the active runway to the runway intersection.
13. Meanwhile, light plane B, which made the go-around, reports on base for 10 at :45.
14. The military plane is now obscured from view of the FSS by a hill.
15. At :47, B makes a touch and go on 10 and is just lifting off again near the runway intersection when the military plane barrels through the intersection on a runway 22 departure.

Radio Refusal ⇒ Near Disaster

From the vantage point of the FSS, the incident was "too close to call. . . . None of the pilots involved complained or talked to the FSS about any of [it] except for the light plane pilot from the first incident [nos. 2 and 4], who happens to be an FSS person."[25]

And even a radio that is being used can be tuned to a wrong or irrelevant frequency. A pilot reports, "We in the air carrier never saw the small twin on approach but we later found out the flight crew had seen us a long way out and had attempted to call us several times [but] we were not on his frequency."[26] A pilot who had not been handed off to the Tower by Approach Control realized that he had not yet received landing clearance and so tried to call Approach Control on his last assigned frequency, which he had not been directed to leave. "No response was received," even though the aircraft was "in the final and critical phases of the approach," but "a large aircraft was . . . sighted (fortunately) in takeoff position on the runway [so] immediate go-around was initiated." As the pilot discovered later, "Tower had been attempting to send us around on their frequency and couldn't understand why I didn't comply."[27]

A controller reports having had to vector three IFR aircraft clear of another aircraft because, inexplicably, "pilot left frequency on his own."[28] Another time, one crew on the wrong frequency "merely 'rogered' descent clearance without giving identification," but "unfortunately [the] clearance was for another aircraft."[29] Yet another pilot was told by Approach Control "to go to Tower frequency" but "misunderstood the frequency and tuned in 118.1 instead of 118.7." While "waiting for a break in conversation on that frequency (118.1) to check in," the aircraft "flew past the approach end of the runway at [its] last assigned heading and altitude."[30]

A civilian pilot reports being "advised by Center that military aircraft were operating to the west at 5,000 feet." While level at 4,000, "we broke out into clear area four to five miles across" and "observed one fighter on the deck northbound." As the pilot "was about to tell Center this, a second fighter dove through my altitude directly ahead of my aircraft and about 250 feet away." It turned out "the military planes were not on Center frequency, common in the area of the occurrence."[31] Another pilot reports, "As decision height, approach light sighting, and threshold sighting occurred, an air carrier was sighted (fortunately) in takeoff position. Immediate go-around. . . . Never occurred to Tower that perhaps I wasn't receiving their transmissions."[32]

Except in cases like the very first example of this chapter, in which "complete electrical failure" occurs, an automatic backup visual communication system of the sort discussed in chapter 11, required in all aircraft and keyed to transponder codes rather than changeable frequencies, would help ameliorate all these sorts of problems by guaranteeing the perpetual availability of at least one communication channel no matter what might be happening with radios.

Problems of Compliance

DISTRACTIONS AND FATIGUE

Just as important as "congested frequencies; several frequencies worked by a single controller; . . . [and] time-consuming repeats of missed or garbled radio transmissions" in undermining successful communication are simple "distractions [and] fatigue."[1] In the words of one controller, reporting a misinterpreted clearance: "Don't know how it happened. Possibly I said ten thousand and wrote down eleven thousand but that doesn't seem likely, although after the day I had, anything could be possible."[2] A pilot, reporting that he had "busted by four or five hundred" an instruction to "descend and maintain 14,000 feet," attributed this to "the day before—good friend to hospital. . . . Late to bed—slept poorly—up early—tired—worried—long flight. . . . Nearly collapsed with exhaustion on way to motel" after landing.[3]

Distractions can prevent a controller from correcting a misunderstood instruction, as in the incident in (157), which somewhat resembles the misunderstanding of *hold* that was seen in (17).[4]

---

(157)
1. Small aircraft A calls on frequency and is cleared to land.
2. Small transport B calls *ready at* 12L *approach end* and is told to *taxi into position and hold* with an aircraft on landing roll.
3. Approach calls on hotline for voice coordination about small aircraft C for landing on runway 12R.
4. Small aircraft A lands approximately 1,000 feet down 12L, *over* small transport B.

Distraction Prevents Controller from Correcting
Misunderstanding

And there can be an aircraft that was cleared to 16,000 feet but that overshoots 16,000 by 600 feet as a result of "distraction as coffee and breakfast entered cockpit"[5] or a crew that misses a frequency change because "at the time the initial call was received the first officer was passing his empty meal tray back and immediately thereafter the captain's meal was passed forward."[6]

An aircraft instructed to climb to 5,000 feet reached 6,500 feet before being challenged by air traffic control because "a passenger asked a question" at 5,000 feet.[7] The Center had to notify another crew that they were "well south of the center line of the airway" because the first officer, who was flying at the time, had been "looking at Mickey Mouse," whose likeness "was plowed in the soil by a farmer and he thought the passengers might enjoy the idea."[8] On another flight an "improper crossing" was brought about by "excess and nonessential communications" on the radio that "broke the chain of thought and concentration of the crew members."[9]

One crew "became involved and never switched from Approach Control to Tower."[10] Another crew, though "instructed to cross at 16,000 or below," instead "crossed at approximately FL 190," because the captain "was getting ATIS and did not monitor [the] F/O."[11] Another captain was "training [a] new copilot and forgot to switch to the tower for landing clearance."[12] Another crew "encountered a bird strike" at 1,500 feet and thus "evidently . . . did not change over to Tower." The first time they recognized that they had landed without a clearance was when Ground Control said (158).[13]

(158)   The Tower says you are cleared to land.

Distraction can lead also to takeoffs without clearance, as when one crew got so involved in verifying checklists that the members forgot to ask for clearance.[14] A pilot, "instructed to call back to Approach while taxiing out to obtain IFR release," recognized the pilot of a small plane as an old friend, taxied out, and made "all the correct calls . . . on the CTAF for the local traffic" but neglected the call to Approach for IFR release "due to short taxi and the conversation with the other pilot. He took off and we followed a short interval later. Once airborne both of us realized we had forgotten to call Approach for release."[15]

Sometimes equipment fails and nobody notices. In an aircraft that had been "cleared to 14,000 feet," a crew member reports, "The altitude selector on the autopilot failed to capture. The altitude alert bell failed to go off. The captain failed to notice for unknown reasons, and I was reading a navigational chart."[16] A controller reports that a pilot whom he had cleared to 17,000 feet but who kept climbing to "175, then 177" explained that he had "overshot a bit" because "he was on autopilot and 'it got away from him.'"[17] Another pilot was cleared to 5,000 feet, climbed at a rate of over 6,000 feet per minute while approaching 4,000 feet, and then leveled at 5,200 feet because "temperature was in the low twenties and the aircraft was light." He acknowledges, "Pilot technique was at fault. . . . I did not expect a vertical performance of that magnitude."[18]

Sometimes disaster is avoided when a controller effectively brings a situation to a distracted crew's attention, in contrast to the ineffective and disastrous example in (54). In one case, with the first officer flying the aircraft, "Center told us we had drifted off course on wrong airway. While correcting, Center advised us we were above our assigned altitude."[19] Sometimes a warning signal does the job. An aircraft with initial clearance to 6,000 feet was given a 180 degree turn at 2,500 feet while it was "climbing in excess of 4,000 feet per minute with a deck angle of twenty degrees nose up," and it was still climbing at that rate when the aural altitude warning signal sounded. The pilot "pushed the airplane over and stopped the climb at 7,000 feet and immediately returned."[20] At other times the warning is not heard but disaster simply chooses not to occur:

> It was a beautiful clear day. Visibility unlimited. When Center called all three crew members were engaged in some activity other than monitoring flight instruments. The captain was looking at a newspaper, the first officer was reading his navigation chart, and the flight engineer was working at his desk. F/O believes he engaged the altitude hold, but we can't be sure. The altitude alert system was working normally, but none of us heard its warning or noticed the yellow light.[21]

And distractions themselves can occasionally have positive consequences. One pilot who had elected to file IFR because of haze had been given clearance "to climb and maintain 2,000 feet."

My front seat passenger was a nonpilot and very interested in viewing the area. As we closed on 2,000 he pointed and asked, "Is that the stadium?" I looked long enough to identify the stadium and when I looked back, the altimeter read 2,060. I throttled back, lowered the nose, lost about fifty feet, and the windshield was immediately filled with another aircraft. The other plane was at 2,000 feet, crossing from my right to my left. It was so close that I could see the color of the pilot's shirt and see that he wore horn-rimmed glasses and a headset. . . . *Had I been precise and on my assigned altitude we would have had a midair.*[22]

However, it would be foolish to count on having such good luck.

IMPATIENCE

Communication effectiveness can also be undermined by impatience. A captain reports hearing on the radio, during a "dark and stormy night" with a "deep stack of aircraft flying around and around west of O'Hare," a "harassed approach controller transmitting almost nonstop," along the lines in (159).

(159)   Global 25, cleared ILS, report the outer marker; Universal 762, descend to eight thousand, report leaving niner, . . .

Suddenly an "impatient voice breaks in with (160), to which the controller responds, "without stopping for breath," along the lines in (161).[23]

(160)   What's our expected approach time? If we hang around here much longer, we'll have to go to Minneapolis.

(161)   Roger, cleared to Minneapolis; Universal 762, you are now cleared for the ILS.

Such rapid clearance delivery is not always the justifiable result of crowded conditions. A pilot reports,

After taxiing out for takeoff and switching to Tower frequency we noticed that the controller repeatedly gave instructions to as many as six aircraft without hardly taking a breath, let alone a pause for a readback or confirmation. We were holding short for several minutes listening to this. Instructions included "cleared for takeoff"; "cleared to land"; "hold short of runway/taxiway"; in addition to traffic conflicts and pattern instructions. Many times this method of communicating seemed unnecessary because the hurried three to six instructions were followed by long periods of silence.[24]

Another pilot suggests:

> It appears to me that too many controllers are issuing clearances like tobacco auctioneers. This includes those on clearance delivery, ground, and local positions, plus approach. Why? If we must ask for a repeat, then all the time saved is lost and the frequency is then overloaded. Don't get me wrong; I can take dictation as fast as anybody, but WHY? Let's reinforce once again that clearances must be smooth and paced in normal, not rushed, manner. This also includes ATIS.[25]

In a reported "story" that has a distinct air of the apocryphal but that obliquely makes the same point, "a southern state copilot . . . was given a very complicated ATC clearance at machine-gun rate." When he asked that the clearance be repeated, "the repeat came back at an even faster rate." At this point the dialogue in (162) to (164) purportedly took place: "The copilot, in a southern drawl, said" (162), got the response (163), and then gave the counterresponse (164).[26]

(162)   Clearance Delivery, do y'all heah how fast ah'm talkin'?

(163)   Affirmative, I do, why?

(164)   That's just about as fast as ah can write, too. Would y'all please repeat the clearance one moah tahm?

Of course, impatience can be dangerous in its own right, even aside from its effect on communication. As one pilot reports, "coming through 700 feet on final I saw the other aircraft take off toward me. I swung right. . . . Pilots should remind themselves that when descending into an uncontrolled airport, they are AT AN UNCONTROLLED AIRPORT."[27]

OBSTINACY AND NONCOOPERATION

And then there are just plain obstinacy and general noncooperation, already seen to have been a major factor in the accident in (17). In another incident, a "pilot of [a] small aircraft was assigned 3,000 feet after departure . . . [and then] was observed through 4,600 feet at which time [a controller] questioned his assigned altitude." It turned out that despite his lower clearance the "pilot had filed for 8,000 and was climbing to that altitude."[28] A "small aircraft on VFR TCA clearance was not happy with being vectored forty miles out of his way for traffic in the metropolitan area." When he came on the controller's frequency, "he made many coarse remarks then finally would not reply to my control instructions or do as he was instructed to do," a refusal that "caused him to come to be in less than standard separation with an air carrier." The controller "tried to turn both aircraft but only the air carrier would comply. This is all that kept the situation from being worse than it was."[29]

Aircraft A, inbound for a visual approach, had to take evasive action to avoid hitting a small aircraft B, diving to 900 feet so "aircraft B passed slightly behind and above." The Tower had given B a turn, but he had not acknowledged. "Later, contact was reestablished with aircraft B and pilot stated the turn was taking him away from his destination so he didn't turn as directed."[30] In another incident, "VFR aircraft A was on delaying vectors for practice approach to runway 10, to follow aircraft B on the ILS 28 approach [but] indicated he did not want to wait for the delay and wanted to return to the airport." Though then advised to plan runway 4, he instead "flew the final to runway 10 into the face of B, who was IFR." When he was given a turn, A "argued that he was VFR and didn't want a vector [but] was told to fly the heading or he was going to hit B. After all this, he finally flew the heading."[31]

A flight instructor was "returning from a cross-country with my student in a small airplane." When they "entered a long downwind for runway 03," he "noticed another small aircraft turn a low crosswind (about 200 feet above the ground), pass under our aircraft, and turn downwind abeam our aircraft." When the instructor "called him and asked if he saw us off his left wing," the other pilot "rocked his wings, presumably acknowledging my call," so the instructor "told him, 'OK, I'll keep it in close for you,'" to which the pilot "made no response nor position report on UNICOM." The instructor "gave right of way to a twin on final approach" and then reported that he "would be turning a short base and final for runway 03," but when he "turned final approach, the other airplane said" (165).

(165)   Hey—you cut us off; I'm ahead of you!

As the instructor "rolled level on final," the other pilot "had turned base early, cutting me off on final approach," so the instructor "had to use an evasive maneuver (approximately fifty-degree bank at 200 feet) and had to go around."[32]

A pilot "told to taxi into position and hold, runway 19," and "aware of another aircraft being told to taxi into position on runway 10 and hold for departing traffic on 19 (us)," was cleared for takeoff and had just rotated, when he heard the Tower tell "the other aircraft to turn left immediately—with heavy emphasis on 'immediately.'" Instead of turning, the other aircraft responded with (166), and "passed over us from three to nine o'clock, about 200 feet above."

(166)   Negative, we want to remain in closed traffic.

As the pilot later learned from the Tower, "the other aircraft mistook our takeoff clearance for their own." He adds, "Confusing two different but similar flight numbers is understandable and even forgivable; refusing to follow traffic controller's commands is not!"[33]

As was seen in chapter 1, the mishap in (17) could have been avoided had the pilot simply followed instructions and gone around when he was first told to. On the other hand, it is sometimes necessary to take initiative, despite the controller's instructions, when the circumstances one finds oneself in obviously and imminently demand it. A pilot found that "If we followed the patterned procedure for the back course we would have been in a very dangerous situation, because it called for a straight ahead path to the OM." He comments, "The MAP obviously never had this situation in mind." As he realized the situation he was in, he "broke off to the left and advised Tower of what I was doing." The Tower "seemed confused [and] told me to make a right turn, which would have placed us head-on to opposite traffic."[34]

FRIVOLOUSNESS AND CREW CONFLICT

Particularly disturbing are incidents that are brought about by frivolousness. A pilot says he "circled airport and made left standard pattern. . . . So much talk on UNICOM that I couldn't talk. People were talking about airport celebration. I told people talking to talk trash on another frequency. One pilot said "Amen," another said, "plane on final is talking to nobody." I replied, "I don't have to." Another pilot told me to stick it in my ear. I told that pilot to stick it in his."[35] Another pilot reports attempting a landing with "my former flight instructor . . . sitting in the back seat and my almost new instructor . . . in the right front seat. Both instructors are real kidders and practical jokers." The pilot remembers hearing the Tower say (167), but he did not then hear (168).

(167)   Turn right at missed approach point for a circle to land on 19.

(168)   Turn right, traffic departing 19. Turn right NOW!

"At this time the instructor in the back seat said, 'PUSH THE NOSE DOWN WE'RE GOING TO HIT THAT AIRPLANE.' The instructor in the right seat then pushed the control yoke forward and most everything in the airplane hit the ceiling. We passed about 180 feet under the airplane, who never saw us." The pilot explains, "I was just too worked up by the instructors and with getting back on course." During the approach "jokes were told and we were talking back and forth pretty freely."[36]

Other pilots report actually having had "jokes" played on them while in flight. In one instance, a pilot, having been cleared to 4,000 feet, mistakenly requested a climb to 7,000 feet on his company frequency and received the reply "climb and maintain 7,000." When he realized he had called on the wrong frequency, he "switched to Departure and asked them to verify" the 7,000 clearance. "The controller said no, but since I was already at 5,400 feet to continue up to 7,000 feet." He adds, "I never discovered the identity of this person who made the reply."[37] In another instance, a flight instructor on a lesson flight was informed upon landing that a military helicopter had followed his aircraft back to the airport,[38] because his transponder was set to 7,700 instead of 1,200. "Someone had set the emergency signal into the transponder prior to our flight and neither my student or I had noticed the error. It was obviously done as a practical joke."

Equally disturbing are incidents that are brought about by conflict within or between crews. A pilot was asked to call a large transport after "Center inadvertently forgot to change this aircraft from low to high altitude frequency" and the controller reporting the incident was "unable to reach it for a frequency change." According to the controller, "He said he would not pass information to the pilot of that particular airline."[39]

A crew member reports being told by the captain, while flying "at approximately FL 180 in a descent, . . . that he was going to try to get me fired. . . . Then ATC cleared us to 16,000 feet. At 15,500 I pulled back on the control yoke to regain the proper altitude."[40] A pilot reports that while his aircraft was crossing the outer marker for landing, the preceding flight announced it "was on the go" and was queried by Approach Control as to the reason for going around. "Reply was that the aircraft ahead was too slow in clearing the runway and had rolled to the end. Another voice then came on the air with the remark, 'Well, he owns it!' The first pilot then launched a diatribe about how the flight was using the runway for a parking spot and that he should have exited the runway sooner and other caustic remarks." While this exchange was still going on, the reporting aircraft landed, realizing only as they turned off the runway that they "were still on Approach frequency."[41]

Some such occurrences appear to be deliberate:

> Tower relayed that another air carrier flight had said smoke was trailing from our right engine. Some smoke is normal—and *such calls are a common form of harassment toward our airline due to employment-related issues.* . . . All indications were normal. . . . The other flight spoke on the Tower frequency in a very sarcastic tone, "Hey, look at that smoke! Whew! That guy sure isn't interested in safety!" . . . Tower immediately called that "it looks fine from here." All this occurred during takeoff roll.[42]

In another incident of false reporting, an aircraft "flew over the airport and reported overhead for left downwind to runway 22," when a "light twin passed under [it] from left to right approximately 300 feet below. No report from him." The aircraft "continued and called left base, at which time the twin called on short final." The pilot of the aircraft "called turning final and saw the twin on a left base leg, not on final as reported, about 500 feet from [it] at the same altitude." The twin "then broke off his left base and landed behind" the aircraft. The pilot continues: "Although not required to report positions at uncontrolled fields, this twin nearly hit us twice and we were looking for him on final, as he reported, even though he was actually on a base leg to the runway. A false report is worse than no report at all! This incident would not have occurred if courtesy had prevailed and the twin had reported his position while approaching to land."[43]

Of course overt rudeness doesn't help either. For one pilot, "During initial handoff from center to Approach all transmissions by controller were so rapid as to be mostly unintelligible. I cautioned him about this shortly after handoff but he totally ignored my request to 'slow down.'" The pilot heard the controller transmit what sounded to him like (169a) but that he later found out was "probably" (169b), "since the airport has no Tower to close IFR."

(169a)   Call inbound.
(169b)   Call on ground.

"On departing the same day the same controller was very rude to the point of screaming on the radio when I tried to call for my IFR clearance for my return flight." He observes, "Single pilot IFR is pretty much a handful and controllers need to be a part of the solution rather than part of the problem."[44]

On the other hand, good crew relations are no guarantee against mistakes or mishaps. A crew member reports having "flown a few trips with this captain before and we trusted each other." As a result, "after we cleared out of 10,000 feet I resumed reading a newspaper and both of us neglected the out of FL 180 callout."[45] In another instance, "the captain was handling the radio communications" and "the first officer, also a qualified captain, was operating the controls from the left seat." When "Center directed the flight to descend," the first officer "misunderstood the clearance" and "set the altitude reminder at FL 240," but "for some reason the captain did not confirm the setting."[46]

General Problems

MESSAGE NOT SENT

Finally, cases can be classified, in general, according as whether necessary information is (a) not sent, (b) sent but not heard, (c) sent and heard but not understood, or (d) sent, heard, and understood but not remembered, even in the absence of other noteworthy particularities. In (170), a case of the first type, the pilot's question reveals that the controller has neglected to tell him that a speed restriction is no longer in effect.[1]

---

(170)
PQR 1939:   Uh they up to speed there at TUV?
—PQR 1939:   Yes sir, you can uh, delete the TUV speed restriction.
   I thought you were at 250 already, sorry.

Controller Forgets to Provide Pilot with Necessary Information

In another case of this type, disaster was barely averted when a crew was not advised of relevant traffic before or after takeoff. "The captain spotted the traffic and pointed it out to the F/O who was flying and nosed the aircraft over into level flight to go under the aircraft fifty to one hundred feet and sightly behind him."[2]

MESSAGE SENT BUT NOT HEARD

A pilot records seeing "what appeared to be another aircraft fly over my left wing in a go-around," after having received a "clearance and taxi instructions for runway 36" and having "crossed runway 27R, using taxiway B. . . . The controller claimed that I acknowledged the hold short order, but I told him that I did not remember [hearing] one and I taxied across the runway not seeing the other aircraft."[3] Another time, a pilot reports, "On approach, a clearance was received to descend from 10,000 to 6,000 and was read back. After leveling at 6,000 for about a minute, the controller said our altitude was supposed to be 7,000 and gave us a sixty-degree left turn. We climbed to 7,000. It appears the readback was missed or went unnoticed by the Approach Control."[4] Another pilot reports being told by a controller "that he had issued 5,000. We told him that we had read back 6,000. He said he did not catch the readback."[5] An aircraft that had been "told to maintain 5,000 feet" and had then "requested 7,000 due to other aircraft going in the same direction" was later "given instructions to climb to 6,000," in response to which the pilot "advised that he was at 7,000 feet" already.[6]

A controller who "gave descent to 15,000 to bizjet due air carrier climbing to 14,000 . . . was forced to issue many additional altitude assignments and radar vectors to avoid loss of separation," because he "did not perceive that pilot of bizjet read back 5,000 feet."[7] Another controller reports, in regard to the near midair collision in (171), "a playback of the tape revealed that the pilot interpreted my traffic information as a clearance . . . [but] I did not hear or acknowledge this."[8]

(171)   Controller: You have crossing traffic at 6,000, two o'clock, ten miles.
Pilot: What's his altitude?
Controller: He's at 6,000.
Pilot: Roger, we're out of 7,000 for 6,000.
Controller: [No response]
Pilot: We just had an airplane go by our nose.
Controller: Roger, that's the traffic I called to you at 6,000.
Pilot: He sure was!

MESSAGE SENT AND HEARD BUT NOT UNDERSTOOD

A pilot who had been instructed to return to 11,000 feet replied "that Center had given him 10,000," but "after reviewing the tape it was clear that he was given 11,000 but had read back 10,000."[9] Another pilot reports a case in which the message got through but was not understood because of an uncertainty in reference of the sort we saw in chapter 2, this time in regard to which airport was intended. The pilot reports that he had "vectored toward the airport . . . used speed brakes and broke out of the clouds with an airport directly ahead . . . cancelled IFR and contacted the flight service station [and] reported downwind, base, and final, only to find *we had landed at the wrong airport*," a result that the pilot attributes to "near identical runway headings, night, close proximity of airports."[10] In a similar incident, a "small aircraft landing on runway 24 made go-around due to a heavy aircraft landing in opposite direction. . . . As it turns out, the heavy had been cleared for visual approach to a nearby airport."[11]

Similar confusions arise from the fact that although "many VORs are located on, or at the boundary of the airport they identify and are named for," there are "some VORs [that] may be situated several miles from an airport with the same name." A captain who interpreted the sequential clearances (172) and (173) as referring to the XYZ VOR found out later from the controller that they had really been intended to be in reference to the XYZ *airport*.

(172)   Cross thirty-five miles out of XYZ at 11,000 feet.

(173)   Cross thirty miles southwest of XYZ at 10,000 feet.

"The XYZ VOR is not colocated with the XYZ airport, an obvious improper clearance if that was his intention."[12]

MESSAGE SENT, HEARD, AND UNDERSTOOD BUT NOT REMEMBERED

A pilot who had been "cleared to cross the VOR at and maintain FL 250" claimed to have read back 240, but later replay of tapes confirmed that he had actually read back (174).[13]

(174)   VOR at 250.

In (175), a controller forgets that he gave a descend instruction (line 12) even though it was sent and acknowledged (line 8), because he confuses it with the same instruction that he gave a little later to someone else (line 9). Note, by the way, the pilot's use of *go ahead* in reference to speaking (line 12), a phrase that was seen to have led to misunderstanding when used with that reference by a controller in (13).[14]

---

(175)

6 (93–97).

—ABC 137 heavy: *Maintain 8,000,* turn right heading uh, 250 to intercept, traffic 12:30 three miles northbound indicating 7,500.

Reply: OK, we're looking for the traffic, and uh, we'll stop at 8, *ABC 137* heavy.

7 (97–99).
—XYZ 543:   Descend and maintain 7,000.
Reply: *Out of seven, we're out of eleven, XYZ 543.*

8 (104–6).
—ABC 425:   *Descend and maintain 7,000.*
ABC 425:   *Leaving eleven for 7,000.*

9 (106–7).
—ABC 137:   You're clear of the traffic now, <u>descend and maintain 7,000</u>
Reply: Down to 7 *ABC 137* heavy.

10 (107–9).
—XYZ 543:   Contact Approach *135.4.*
Reply: *35.4* Good day, *XYZ 543.*

11 (114–16).
ABC 137 heavy: Contact Approach *135.65.*
Reply: *35.65* Good day sir.

12 (118–26).
—ABC 425:   *ABC 425—Airport,* Go ahead.
Reply: Um, *I don't remember giving you lower,* <u>I gave your company about ten miles ahead of you lower,</u> however.
ABC 425:   Uh, *you gave us down to seven, we acknowledged.*
Reply: Uh, *maybe I did call you,* anyway *maintain 7,000* present heading intercept the 095 radial.
—ABC 425:   OK, *descend to 7.*

Controller Forgets Having Given an Instruction

In another incident of this type, an aircraft at 2,000 feet after takeoff was told by Departure Control "to maintain 250 knots in climb," but after leaving 10,000 feet, the aircraft "accelerated to normal climb (300 knots)." The reporting pilot "forgot, and copilot either forgot or did not notice the airspeed deviation from 250 knots after leaving 10,000 feet."[15]

Another time, an automatically provided default value was inadvertently allowed to override an explicit verbal restriction. The pilot was told "to maintain less than 250 knots," but "passing over 10,000 feet the computer generated optimum speed bug moved to 295 knots climbing speed and, forgetting the restriction," the pilot "accelerated while climbing." When questioned by the Center, he "then remembered the restriction, apologized, and slowed back to 250."[16] And another pilot reports, "Clearance was received on the ground to maintain 250 K until further advised [but] upon leaving 10,000 a normal acceleration to 310 K was made. Departure control requested our speed and we immediately reduced to 250 K." The pilot observes, "We have been accelerating at 10,000 feet for a long time" and suggests, "It seems that with this new procedure at some airports of maintaining 250 until advised it would be a good practice for Departure Control to remind you of that clearance as you leave the frequency."[17]

Part III

Potential Solutions

Immediate Fixes

As the pilot quoted at the end of chapter 8 implies, there are steps that can be taken immediately to ameliorate the sorts of problems examined in parts 1 and 2. A pilot who "read back 3,000 to the controller" and was later told he "was only cleared to 3,600" suggests that "controllers should place more importance on *what the pilot thinks he hears.*"[1] The controller who reports the following incident concurs: "Air carrier checked on frequency climbing to FL 230. I THOUGHT I told him to maintain 230 and I issued a military aircraft at FL 240 as his traffic, telling the air carrier that he could expect higher when clear. Inadvertently, I issued him clearance to maintain the same altitude as his traffic. . . . The air carrier read back my initial clearance, 'Okay.'" He suggests, "I would emphasize to controllers the importance of listening precisely to clearances issued and requiring pilots to read back clearances other than as 'Okay.'"[2] Put more generally, "clearances should be read back, and . . . the readbackee should pay attention *to make sure that his communication has been received accurately* by the readbackor."[3]

A pilot who "thought he was issued (176) but was then told (177), upon reaching 22,300 feet, makes the converse suggestion.

(176)   Converging traffic; descend to 220.

(177)   Climb back to FL 230.

"I *should have been more alert* to possible misunderstanding and *questioned the controller* further. We found out the other traffic was at 220."[4]

Sometimes the responsibility is shared. One pilot reports, "Cleared for the visual, our final approach controller failed to turn us over to the Tower and we failed to contact them until after clearing the runway."[5] The pilot who reported the incident involving (144) and (145) also points to a joint responsibility for correcting such problems. He suggests that "controllers use the words 'heading,' 'degrees,' 'flight level,' 'airspeed,' etc., when giving instructions which include numbers," and adds "closer listening by flight crew and requesting verification if in doubt prior to taking any action."

Further steps that can be taken include shorter shifts, more staff, better equipment, and—most significantly in the present context—broader training, the latter aimed especially at increasing the awareness of controllers, pilots, and crews of the nature and seriousness of such problems and of the need to be constantly on the lookout for them. In the words of one air traffic control supervisor, "As with any problem, *awareness* is the first key. Controllers, be aware of your propensity not to listen with full attention to readbacks. Pilots, if you didn't hear that instruction, don't guess, ask for a repeat. Next, include erroneous readbacks at every level of air traffic training so developmental controllers don't start down this road" of getting "'trained' to get correct readbacks" and thus to think that "the time spent listening to readbacks can be used to plan and formulate [further] clearances," rather than for checking to make sure pilots have correctly heard the clearances that have already been given to them.[6]

Much of what we take for granted about language and communication in everyday life is simply false. The processes through which people communicate and understand each other are much more complex than they superficially appear to be. Training should include some sophisticated discussion of the social and cognitive aspects of these processes and the ways these aspects can interact to lead the processes themselves awry, as revealed in the examples in this book.

A Long-Term Solution:
An Intelligent Voice Interface
for Aviation Communication

A close to ideal solution to at least some of the sorts of problems discussed in previous chapters would be the development of an intelligent voice interface for aviation communication. Such a device would monitor communications and filter out potential linguistic confusions, checking with the speaker for clarification before conveying messages and monitoring the aircraft's state, providing needed callouts automatically. Such a system would be valuable on line, as a safety device in real time, but would be useful also as a training device along the lines mentioned at the end of chapter 9, an aid to developing an awareness in both pilots and controllers of the kinds of linguistic constructions they ought to avoid while conditioning them, to some extent, to do so.

The general structure of such a system, as it would function in the air traffic controller/pilot communication circuit, is shown in figure 1. Each speaker would speak, as usual, into a microphone, but the message would be filtered through an intelligent voice input component and inspected for linguistic problems before being conveyed; the system would check back with the speaker via an intelligent voice output component, when explicit clarification is needed. The intelligent voice output component would serve the further function of guaranteeing that required call-outs and readbacks are provided, by providing them itself when necessary. The intelligent voice input component would also have potential, incidentally, for mediating voice communications between humans and machines, as outlined in figure 2.

The intelligent voice input component would consist of two subcomponents—the voice word recognizer, in which raw speech would be deciphered into meaningful linguistic patterns, and the language filter, in which disambiguation, refer-

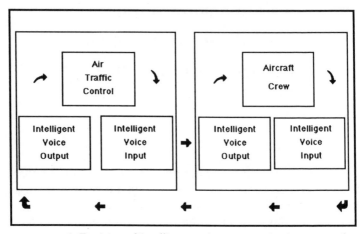

FIGURE 1: Envisioned intelligent voice communication network for air traffic control

ence determination, and other interpretive decisions would be made—and it would feed its results into the intelligent voice output component, as shown in figure 3. The language filter would incorporate the five components of an ideal natural language understanding system shown in figure 4, the lexicon, syntax, semantics, and pragmatics of the language in question—aviation English in the present setting—and the general nonlanguage knowledge base that would be expected to be available to the intended users of the system, including knowledge of aviation and related matters for a system intended for pilots and controllers.

A lexicon of a language is a formal description of its vocabulary, consisting of one or more entries for each word, specifying its meanings and its grammatical and pronunciation

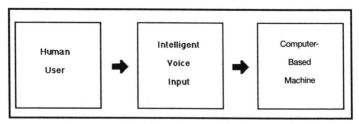

FIGURE 2: Envisioned intelligent human machine voice interface

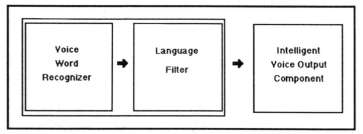

FIGURE 3: The subcomponents of the intelligent voice input component

peculiarities as well as an account of the regularities that relate different words and any exceptions to those regularities. For example, a lexicon for ordinary English would specify that *dog* can be a noun, an adjective, or a transitive verb, as in (178a, b, and c), whereas *canary* can be a noun or an adjective but not a transitive verb, as indicated by the contrast between the sentences (179a) and (179b), on the one hand, and the nonsense nonsentence (and therefore *-marked) word string (179c), on the other.

(178a)   Fido is a dog.
(178b)   Fido eats dog food.
(178c)   Fido loves to dog Tweety.

(179a)   Tweety is a canary.
(179b)   Tweety eats canary seed.
(179c)   *Tweety loves to canary Fido.

A lexicon for English would also specify such relations between or among words as that adding the suffix -*r* to a verb that ends in -*e* (e.g., *dine* ⇒ *diner*) or adding -*er* to any other verb (e.g., *eat* ⇒ *eater*) produces a noun that means one who performs the action specified by that verb, as well as such facts as that *diner* has an alternative related meaning as a kind of place where one dines and that *liver* has two altogether unrelated meanings as an organ and a kind of bird.[1] A lexicon can be structured formally as a list, a network, or some more complicated algebraic system and implemented computationally in various ways.[2]

A syntax of a language is a formal specification of its grammatical patterns, the rules or principles that determine the relative degrees of grammaticality of arbitrary strings of

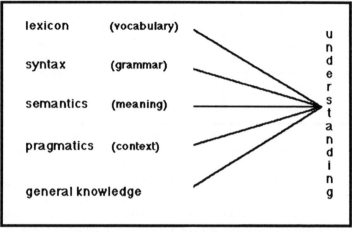

FIGURE 4: The five components of language understanding

words. For example, the four word strings in (180) all contain exactly the same words, but while (180a) and (180b) are both grammatical sentences of ordinary English—though differing substantially in meaning, a fact not relevant to grammaticality—(180c) is not a complete sentence but can begin one (for example, when followed by *is an experimental model*) and (180d) is gibberish.

(180a)   The pilot flew the plane.
(180b)   The plane flew the pilot.
(180c)   *The plane the pilot flew.
(180d)   *The the flew plane pilot.

Just as a lexicon identifies the words of a language and their properties and interrelationships as words, a syntax characterizes the grammatical constructions that can occur in a language, that is, the ways words can form combinations, from the simplest phrases to the most complex complete sentences. Like a lexicon, a syntax can be structured to varying degrees of complexity, containing rules or principles of different possible forms, and can be implemented computationally in various ways.[3]

A semantics of a language is a formal specification of how meaning is conveyed by the sentences of the language. For example, in English, as in many other languages, meaning is conveyed largely by word order, as shown in (181), which contains four different arrangements of exactly the same words.

(181a)   The man sees the woman.
(181b)   The woman sees the man.
(181c)   *The man the woman sees.
(181d)   *The woman the man sees.

Both (181a) and (181b) are meaningful sentences, but they have opposite meanings relative to who is doing the seeing and who is being seen, whereas (181c) and (181d) are meaningless when taken as full sentences. In Latin, by contrast, as in many other languages, word order is relatively unimportant to meaning, because meaning is conveyed instead by inflections—prefixes and suffixes that attach to the roots of words—as in the examples in (182) and (183).

(182a)   Vir videt feminam.
(182b)   Vir feminam videt.
(182c)   Feminam vir videt.
(182d)   Feminam videt vir.

(183a)   Femina videt virum.
(183b)   Femina virum videt.
(183c)   Virum femina videt.
(183d)   Virum videt femina.

Each of the examples in (182) is synonymous with—has the same meaning as—(181a), and each of the examples in (183) is synonymous with (181b), despite the differences in word order, because in Latin it is the absence or presence of the final -*m* in *virum* ("man") or *feminam* ("woman") that indicates whether the mentioned person is the doer or the receiver, respectively, of the seeing (*videt*), regardless of where in the sentence the relevant noun occurs.[4] How best to structure a semantics formally is still an open question of scientific linguistic research.[5]

A pragmatics of a language is a formal specification of how its use and understanding are affected by context. For example, the sentence (184) will be understood as synonymous with (185a) when asked at a recycling center, but it will be understood as synonymous with (185b) when asked at the cash register of a restaurant.

(184)   Do you take plastic?
(185a)   Do you accept plastic items for recycling?
(185b)   Do you accept credit cards as payment?

Similarly, the sentence (186) has one meaning when uttered in a discussion of one's work schedule and quite a different meaning when uttered while pulling one's car into a metered parking space.

(186)   I have some free time.

And even the seemingly syntactic issue of what constitutes a full sentence can be strongly affected by context. To hear the otherwise nonsentence word string (187) uttered in isolation would generally be perplexing unless one were standing in the checkout line of a supermarket, in which case one would understand it immediately as a full question about what kind of bag or sack one wants the groceries placed in.

(187)   A paper or a plastic?

How best to deal formally with the relevant sorts of facts is even more of an open question for pragmatics than is the corresponding question for semantics and is one of the most intensively studied areas of current linguistic research.[6]

A knowledge base for the language filter of an intelligent voice interface would contain the extralinguistic domain-specific real-world knowledge that the intended users of the system could reasonably be expected or required to possess. Such language-independent factual knowledge can be crucial in drawing implicit inferences correctly, in disambiguating sentences that have more than one meaning, in determining the references of pronouns in unclear cases, and even in determining the appropriate context for interpreting a particular utterance.

In a system intended for use in air traffic control, the knowledge base would have to include all information concerning actual flights and the air traffic control environment that would be needed to clarify linguistic or nonlinguistic communication-related confusion. In contrast to the general examples given in this chapter purely for expository purposes, the content of the knowledge base and of the other four components would have to be derived, in large part, from actual examples of aircraft/air traffic control dialogue, such as the accident-related examples discussed in earlier chapters. Exactly how such knowledge is to be collected, structured, organized, and processed remains to be seen, as research in this area continues to progress.[7] The only certainty is that a workable intelligent voice interface is a very long-term goal, not likely to be developed for this generation of aviation or the next.

A Shorter-Term Solution:
An Error-Resistant Visual Interface
for Aviation Communication

Though not likely to be perfected very soon, systems of the sort discussed in the preceding chapter will become increasingly feasible as more is learned about semantics and pragmatics, as more effective ways of organizing and processing knowledge representations are developed, and as the technology for speech recognition—for extracting meaningful linguistic representations from acoustic signals—becomes more sophisticated. In the meantime and in parallel with that research, it may be fruitful to develop more limited systems, in which a visual interface for processing a more restricted English-like language is used.[1] A prototype version of such a system, the Aviation Interface Research (AIR) System, developed under my supervision by some of my graduate students at Boston University, is described in this chapter. Technical details of the system are given in the appendix.

AIR uses a system of nested menus to send messages back and forth between two Macintosh computers, which simulate pilot and controller interfaces as illustrated schematically at the software block level in figure 5. When a message is entered from one of these two user interfaces, the respective parser program checks it for well-formedness—grammaticality with respect to the restricted English-like language used by the system—before permitting it to be transmitted to the other interface, where it appears at the top of the screen; if necessary, an error message is returned to the sender instead. Menu screens are invoked by selecting symbolic icons, and messages are constructed by selecting buttons that contain actual words or phrases, which are echoed at the bottom of the sending screen. The typical screen layout is illustrated schematically in figure 6. As the system is implemented at present, the selections are made by mouse, but they could just as well be made,

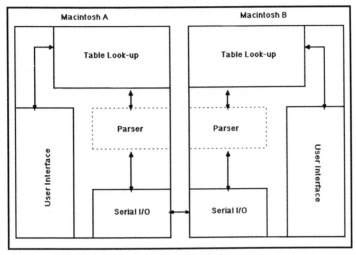

FIGURE 5: AIR System software block diagram

more realistically, by touchscreen. A sample of the sorts of messages that the present parser will recognize as well formed and permit to be sent is given in figure 7.

The actual message-sending process is illustrated, for the controller's interface, in figures 8–13. The pilot's interface is similar. Figure 8 shows the top-level screen, which provides four options: *general messages, clearance instructions, traffic information,* and *emergencies.* Each of these options invokes a new screen, in which outgoing messages of the selected sort can be constructed. As in all of the screens, incoming messages appear in the upper portion of the screen. The outgoing message appears, as its parts are chosen, in the lower portion. This portion is not used at this level but is shown for screen consistency. The *show parse tree* option is a development aid that enables the developer to examine the syntactic structure of the message as it is being built. This would be of little utility to an end user and would most likely not be provided in a deployed system.

Figure 9 shows one of the windows that can be invoked from the top-level screen in figure 8. The controller can instruct the pilot to squawk a transponder code or to turn in one or another direction or to stop a turn or can choose among other options for further message choices. The *type in text* option enables the

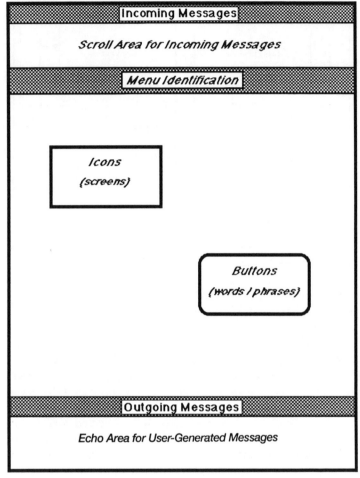

FIGURE 6: Typical AIR System screen design

user to augment the message with further information if necessary. If a message is completed at this level, it can be sent by pressing the *over* button, which also returns the system to the top-level screen.

Figure 10 shows the screen that is invoked by selecting the *low altitude alert* option in figure 9. Choosing any one of the six options available at this level invokes the next-level screen, shown in figure 11, which provides for the selection of a desired altitude or (equivalently) flight level. The part of the message that has been constructed thus far now appears in the *outgoing messages* window at the bottom of this newly invoked screen.

Selecting either of the *flight level* or *altitude* options in the screen in figure 11 adds the corresponding text to the outgoing message and invokes the keypad screen shown in figure 12, in which the desired number is selected. Touching the *done* button in the screen in figure 12 adds the selected number to the outgoing message and returns to the screen in figure 11. Touching the *done* button in the reinvoked screen in figure 11 (with the altitude or flight level now added to the outgoing message) returns the system to the screen shown in figure 13—that is, the low altitude alert screen of figure 10, but with the complete message now shown in the *outgoing messages* portion of the screen. Touching the *over* button in this screen sends the message, clears the bottom of the screen, and returns the

---

Weather area between 1 o'clock and 3 o'clock 7 miles.

4 mile band of chaff from 10 miles south of Boston VORTAC to 20 miles north of Baltimore VORTAC.

Traffic alert 9 o'clock, 5 miles, eastbound, converging. Advise you turn right heading 045 and climb to flight level 190 immediately.

Hold short of runway.

Flock of geese, 6 o'clock 4 miles northbound, last reported at altitude 15 thousand 7 hundred.

Contact Logan ground 131.1.

Wind shear alerts all quadrants. Centerfield wind north at 30 knots varying to northeast at 20 knots.

Maintain flight level 203 10 miles past Chicago VORTAC.

Reduce speed by 30 knots.

Descend and maintain altitude 16 thousand 3 hundred. Then reduce speed by 10 knots.

FIGURE 7: Examples of messages accepted for transmission by the AIR System

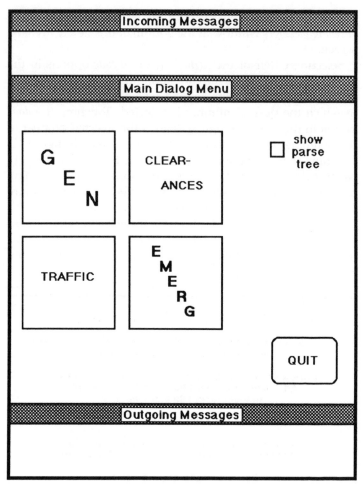

FIGURE 8: AIR System top-level screen

system to the top-level screen of figure 8, ready to construct and send the next message.

As it now stands, AIR serves mainly to illustrate the concept and demonstrate the feasibility of an error-resistant visual message-sending and receiving system for two-way air-ground, pilot-controller communication. A second version is under development that will improve on the current version in several ways. In particular, the current version was developed using two Unix-based compiler-development tools, LEX and

BISON, that were very helpful in getting the project going but that restrict the user in various ways that do not necessarily improve the efficiency of the resulting system. The new version is being developed from scratch to increase flexibility and make full use of available computational power.

The system is envisioned as having several further features that are not present in the current version, three of which are

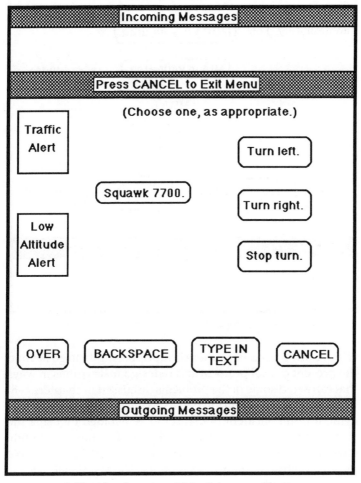

FIGURE 9: Next-level screen with both icons and buttons

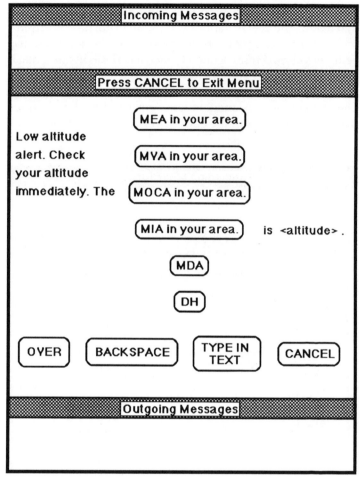

FIGURE 10: Screen invoked by *low altitude alert* icon in figure 9

worth noting here. First, there is the opportunity to go beyond the present official protocol and redesign instructions in ways that can avoid some of the problems discussed in chapters 1–8. For example, the confusion between *climb* and *descend* that was evident in the incident in (34) could be avoided by using the single phrase *change altitude*, with the direction of altitude change indicated by numerical parameters, as in the sample possible instruction shown in figure 14. The first <<*altitude*>> parameter would serve as a check on the current position of the aircraft and could be questioned by a pilot who thinks it is incorrect. The second <<*altitude*>> parameter is the one that is given in current *climb* or *descend* instructions as the altitude to be achieved through the execution of the instruction. The difference between *climb* and *descend* is embodied in the relative values of the two parameters, without the controller or pilot needing to understand the idiosyncratic antonymy (opposite) relation between these two particular English verbs or to remember which is which. Further instructions that might be

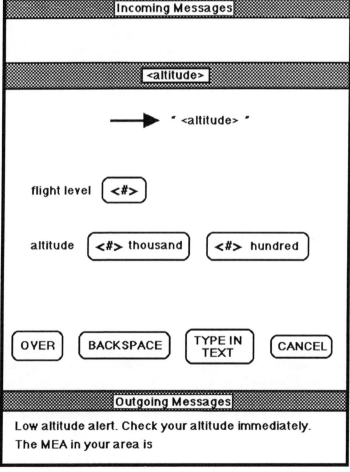

FIGURE 11: Screen showing partial message constructed thus far

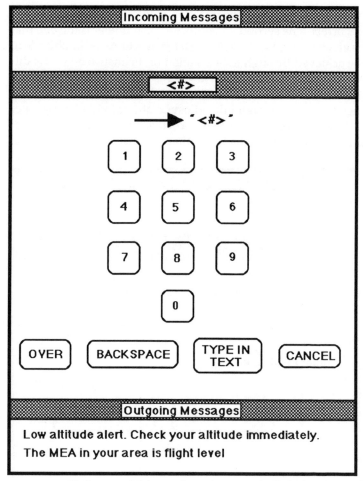

FIGURE 12: Screen with keypad to select specific flight level

candidates for redesign are the various *taxi to* and *hold short* combinations, which can lead to confusions such as those seen in (27) to (29) and (53).[2]

Second, there is the possibility of providing bilingual screens, in English and in the user's own language, to enable the crew or controller to check the correctness of messages they want to send or test their understanding of messages they receive. The problems involved in machine translation for an entire language, including the full range of available grammatical constructions and imagistic devices such as tropes and metaphors, are at present still next to intractable, for essentially the same reasons as for the system outlined in chapter 10, but the corresponding problem for a suitably restricted literal fragment of a language, such as the aviation communication protocol, perhaps with some redesign, is relatively simple. The ability to invoke a screen in one's own language that is exactly equivalent to the one being used by one's interlocutor in a

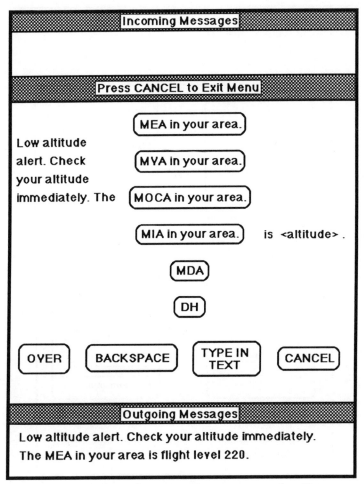

FIGURE 13: Screen of figure 10 with message completed by selections in screens of figures 11 and 12

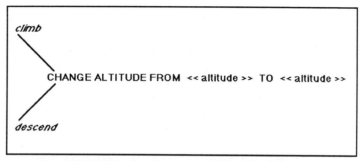

FIGURE 14: Possible redesigned instruction to avoid cross-language verb confusions

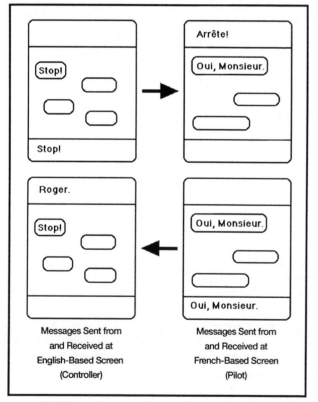

FIGURE 15: Bilingual screens for sending or receiving messages in different languages

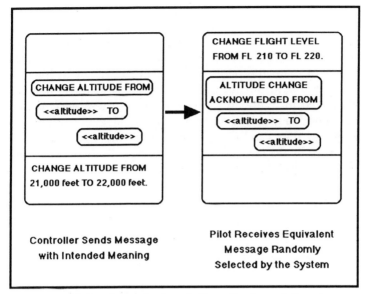

Random selection of alternative formulations to prevent boredom from ritualistic repetition

different language, as illustrated in figure 15, would make it possible to avoid the whole range of cross-language confusions of the sort discussed in chapter 4.

Furthermore, this feature would help nonnative speakers of English keep track of near-homophonous clearance instructions whose usage differs in different places, such as those in (188), assuming those clearances do not get redesigned.

(188a)   Position and hold.
(188b)   Hold position.
(188c)   Hold your position.

The clearance in (188a) "can be applied quite differently in Europe than in the United States," and European controllers can apparently use (188b) to express a meaning similar to the one United States controllers use (188c) to express. Having all of this clarified automatically in the receiver's own language can only help to ameliorate an otherwise formidable terminological tangle.[3]

Finally, there is the option mentioned at the end of chapter 4, in which a specific formulation of an instruction is chosen randomly from a set of synonymous alternative formulations in order to prevent the boredom that is induced by repeatedly receiving instructions of exactly the same form. For example, the controller could send an instruction of the form shown in figure 14, with the pilot receiving an equivalent instruction in a different formulation chosen randomly by the system, as illustrated in figure 16. The controller can rest assured that the intended meaning will get across to the pilot unchanged, while the pilot can be confident of receiving that meaning as intended by the controller without being lulled to sleep by the hypnotic repetition of exactly the same words.

Appendix

The Aviation Interface Research (AIR) System:
Technical Description

CONTENTS

A1. Introduction

This appendix explains the operation and support of the Aviation Interface Research (AIR) System, which was developed to explore methods of enhancing the effectiveness of DATALINK, a communications link between air traffic control stations and aircraft that is projected by the Federal Aviation Administration (FAA) to be deployed during the 1990s. DATALINK will make it possible to replace or supplement current voice communications with visual and written instructions.

The prototype communication system described here consists of unambiguous, context-free grammars based on the current air traffic control language and Macintosh-based visual interfaces that accomplish several tasks. The interfaces demonstrate the developing lexicons, exercise the lexicons in a realistic context, and facilitate discussion of how the instructions composed of elements of the lexicons might be presented visually to pilots and controllers.

Two separate programs for the AIR System were developed, one providing for a controller grammar, lexicon, and interface and the other providing for a pilot grammar, lexicon, and interface. The two programs, run on separate displays, demonstrate the two sides of the AIR system. The physical DATALINK is simulated with a standard NULL modem serial link that allows messages to be passed between these two sides. This appendix describes primarily the controller side of the AIR System, hereafter called "the system." The pilot side, mentioned here only occasionally in passing, is similar.

Prototypes are valuable because they can reveal hidden issues and demonstrate the feasibility of some design choices and the infeasibility of others. Although the actual visual interface of an eventually deployed DATALINK communication system may bear little resemblance to the prototype discussed here, this model raises ergonomic issues that may constrain the lexicon, the grammar, or the interface design of such an actual system.

A2. System Requirements

The AIR System runs on two Macintosh II computers with at least one megabyte of memory each. The two computers are connected via a twenty-five-pin NULL modem serial cable, with a Macintosh modem cable attached to the serial cable at each end. The THINK C compiler, version 4.0, distributed by Symantec Corporation, was used for program development. ResEdit version 1.2 or 2.0 was used for developing the resource files. The Unix-based compiler development tools LEX and BISON were used to develop the parsers.

A3. THE HUMAN INTERFACE
A3.1 Overview

The system partitions the Macintosh screen into three rectangular windows at each of several levels. The uppermost of these windows at each level, the *incoming messages window,* displays incoming messages from the other side of the system (for the controller; messages from the pilot at the other end of the link). The middle window, the *menu window,* contains a collection of menus (not to be confused with Macintosh pull-down menus) representing various topics in the air traffic protocol (e.g., clearances, traffic advisories, flight instructions). It is the menu window that allows valid air traffic control messages to be entered. The bottom window, the *outgoing messages window,* displays the outgoing message as it is entered.

The menu window has been designed to accomplish the complementary tasks of limiting the number of menu levels and preventing any one menu from becoming too cluttered with information. A menu at the top or second level may therefore have a series of submenus that provide access to messages based on general categories marked by icons. The menu window also contains buttons, which are used for selecting text or text types in the process of constructing messages.

A3.2 Icons and Buttons

Icons are used to access other menus at levels below the current menu. They can be thought of as identifying categories of messages that are waiting to be found behind them. They do not contain any text that will become part of the outgoing message. *Buttons,* in contrast, provide the means of building the actual text of the outgoing message. There are two types of buttons: *dialogue buttons,* which provide access to the actual phrases that make up the lexicon, and *command buttons,* which perform special functions for changing, correcting, or canceling the sentence currently being built.

The user selects an icon or button by a single mouse click. The use of a mouse could be, and indeed is intended to be, replaced eventually by a touchscreen. The keyboard is not used in this touchscreen simulation (except in a special debugging *type in text* mode that would not be part of a deployed system).

When a command button is clicked, the command is performed. Available command buttons include *cancel* and *erase message* to destroy the current message, *backspace digit* and *backspace window* to make changes in the middle of a message, *done* to indicate the end of a numeric entry, and *over* to send the completed message to the parser and transmit it if correct. There are also several debugging command buttons, including *type in text*, *show parse tree*, and *show debug info*. Finally, there is a pull-down menu containing a special *quit* selection to allow the simulation to be terminated.

When a dialogue button is clicked, the text contained in the button is processed. In an earlier version of the system, a button simply contained text that was added to the message in the output message window. To limit the number of buttons on the screen at any given time, however, the processing of text received from the selection of a button has been made more sophisticated. A single dialogue button may cause multiple actions to occur. In addition to placing text in the output messages window, a button can reveal another menu consisting of other buttons. These are called *bracketed dialogue buttons*, because the text in the button is surrounded by angle brackets, as in *<direction>*. By nesting buttons in this manner, the system leads the user through the message by providing only valid phrases whenever possible. But there are still dialogue buttons that allow incorrect phrases to be entered, as listed in section A8.4. A dialogue button may also have embedded command buttons. This saves user time by allowing commands to be executed automatically wherever necessary.

A3.3 Alert Dialogue Boxes

Alert dialogue boxes are windows that provide information about the system itself or indicate an error. The *about* alert dialogue box lists the name, version number, and completion date of the system. The *parse fail* alert dialogue box is displayed whenever the parser returns an error status. The *unk button* alert dialogue box is displayed when a button the user has pressed has not been provided by the system developers in the current version. This should not be necessary in a deployed system.

A3.4 Error Detection

Errors are detected as they occur while the outgoing message is built. This is accomplished by sending the entire message, as it stands at each step of its construction, to the parser as each level of menu is entered. At any time, if a subphrase of the message is found to be syntactically incorrect, the system responds with an alert dialogue box that identifies the errant subphrase and waits for the user to click the OK button. After the user acknowledges the error, the system automatically removes the incorrect text and redisplays the menu corresponding to the place where the error occurred.

A4. Program Development and Organization

The system software was built around a public domain application skeleton called TransSkel. The TransSkel package provided the basic tools to manipulate Macintosh windows and to respond to events. TransSkel (and the system itself) was based on the THINK C version 4.0 (formerly Lightspeed C) compiler for the Macintosh computer. THINK C provides a C development environment for the Macintosh; the use of the compiler and the environment is explained in the THINK C documentation. Generally, C programs are organized as entities called projects in the THINK C vernacular and are indicated by an icon of a black square within a white square. Double clicking a project icon will reveal a series of menus and a list of program modules in the project (a project is a single linked piece of code).

The system consists of three major pieces: an engine, a parser, and a resource file. The engine, starting with the main module *datalink.c*, is responsible for overall control of the simulation. As such, it displays and interprets icons and menus and builds sentences for the parser based on user-selected buttons. It can be termed an engine because it knows little or nothing about the contents of a given menu.

The parser, created using the Unix-based compiler development tools LEX and BISON, matches the input message against a set of syntax rules to determine if the message is acceptable. If an error is detected, the parser returns a pointer to the errant text. Whenever changes to the syntax are desired, the new rules must be entered and the parser must be regenerated in the Unix environment. Then a number of changes to the parser must be made to make it compatible with the Macintosh-based AIR System. This is described in detail in the section on the parser. See figure A1 for an overview of the system design.

All menus and icons displayed by the AIR System are contained in two Macintosh resource files. The resource file for the controller side is called *datalink.proj.rsrc*. The resource file for the pilot side is called *pilot.proj.rsrc*. The contents of these files can be altered or completely replaced to produce entirely different results when processed by the AIR program. It is important to remember that the parser must be updated to match the resource file.

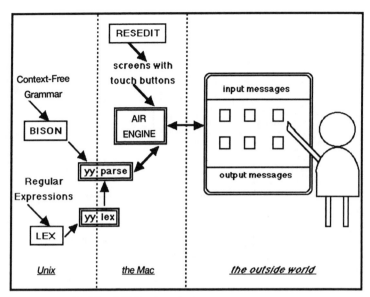

FIGURE A1: The AIR System design

A5. THE ENGINE
A5.1 Overview

The system engine is responsible for overall control. It displays and interprets icons and menus contained in a resource file and builds sentences for the parser based on user-selected buttons. As an engine, it knows how to display the menus, but it knows nothing generally about the contents of menus. See figure A2 for an overview of the engine design.

The engine operates through a series of menus that call various levels of the menu window, which takes up the middle portion of the screen and provides for all the text necessary to create phrases through the use of icons and buttons, as discussed in section A3. When a menu selection is chosen, its level of the menu window overlays any previous level that may already be displayed.

In addition to the menu window with its various levels, two specialized windows exist, each consisting only of a static text box, one that takes up the top part of the screen and one that occupies the bottom. The window at the top of the screen displays incoming messages received from the other AIR program (from the pilot, for the controller side). The window at the bottom of the screen displays outgoing mes-

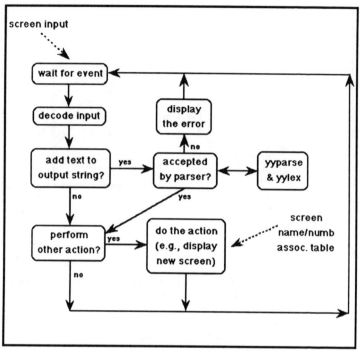

FIGURE A2: The AIR System engine design

sages that are constructed as the user moves through the various layers of menus.

A5.2 EVENT PROCESSING

The primary purpose of the engine is to wait for events and then process them, displaying menus, placing text in the outgoing message, or both. An event is generated by any mouse click by the user. A subroutine called *event* determines the type of event and takes the appropriate action. The subroutine determines if the event was selected with an icon or a button. In the case of an icon, a mask is used to determine the ID of the menu to be displayed, and the menu is then displayed. In the case of a button, a *process_button* subroutine is called to determine the appropriate action.

A button contains a text string, some of which may be displayed in the button and some of which may be hidden from the viewer. Processing the text in a button involves dividing it into text for the output string and commands for the button processer. The text string is appended to the message being formed and displayed in the outgoing message window. Whenever the text string has a word in angle brackets—for example, *<direction>*—this indicates that when that button is pressed, the menu whose name is bracketed—*direction* in this case—will pop up for the user to choose an option (in this case a direction) and then continue with the rest of the message. After the text of a button has been completed, including any embedded commands, the entire message entered so far is sent to the parser. If the partial message parse is successful, the message is continued. If the partial message parse results in an error, an alert dialogue box is displayed describing the error.

Commands are acted on as they occur. Once the appropriate action is taken, the engine waits for the next event to occur. The currently supported commands and what they do are as follows:

OVER	Signals that the outgoing message text should be parsed and then sent out if the parse is successful. An unsuccessful parse will generate an alert dialogue box.
BACKSPACE DIGIT	Causes the most recently entered digit to be deleted from the outgoing message.
BACKSPACE WINDOW	Causes the most recently entered text subphrase to be deleted from the outgoing message and then displays the appropriate menu, where the deleted fragment can be reentered or corrected.
DONE	Causes control to return to the next higher-level menu.
ERASE MESSAGE	Causes the entire message entered thus far to be erased.
CANCEL	Causes the entire message to be erased and returns to the menu immediately below the main menu.
TYPE IN TEXT	Special debugging command button that allows the user to enter text from the keyboard.
SHOW PARSE TREE	Special check box on the main menu that can be activated to display a parser tree when the outgoing message is completed.
SHOW DEBUG INFO	Special check box on the main menu that can be activated to display information to aid the programmer in debugging.

QUIT   Special Macintosh pull-down menu on the
                                main menu that allows for termination of a
                                message-sending session.

A5.3 Engine Startup Procedure

When the system is started up, the engine performs several initialization procedures. Among these are initialization of all of the dialogue
buttons and boxes in the resource file and initialization of the tables
needed by the parser.

The dialogues, obtained from the resource file, are initialized in two
ways. Most are initialized by reading their resource IDs from a table in
the file *dialogdesc.c*. A few special dialogues exist that have IDs that are
hard coded into the engine. These are the main menu, the incoming
messages window, the outgoing messages window, the parse tree
window, and all the alert dialogue boxes.

A5.4 Engine Subroutines

The main routine of *datalink.c* is near the bottom of the file. This routine does some initialization. In addition to it and the *event* routine, a
number of other routines exist within *datalink.c.*:

SetDCtl   Turns the debug check box on/off in the
                                main menu.
SetDText   Sets the string in a dialogue's static text.
pprintf   Replaces printf; used to write text to
                                dialogue box instead of console.
addchar_ifnot_insidenumber
                                Used to put blanks or other characters
                                between words but not within numbers.
safe_strncat   Concatenates some number *n* of characters
                                if, and only if, the resultant string ≤ 252
                                characters.
safe_strcat   Concatenates to a string if, and only if, the
                                resultant string ≤ 252 characters.
substr   A fancy substring that removes multiple
                                blanks, if requested.
divide_3ways   Divides a string into up to three parts,
                                depending upon the parameters and the
                                values found in the string.
display_incoming   Prints received serial data in a dialogue
                                window.
display_dialog_and_print
                                Uses display_this_dialog to display a dialog
                                and puts string into item in dialogue.

display_this_dialog	Displays a requested bracketed dialogue at the next unused level.
remove_blanks_at_end	
	Removes trailing blanks from end of a Pascal string, stores adjusted length in the first byte of string, and adds \O after last character of string.
process_button	Processes the text string received from a button.
Close	Closes a dialogue box.
Clobber	Removes dialogue resource and closes.
DoFileMenu	Handles the file menu at screen top.
DoAbout	Handles a selection under the Apple menu *about datalink*.
DemoDialog	Sets up first level dialogues (menus).
TmpDialog	Creates second- and third-level dialogues (menus).
OpenSerial	Opens the serial communications port.
GetData	Gets incoming serial data into a local buffer.
SendData	Outputs successfully parsed messages to a serial port.

In addition to these local routines, some routines are found in the TransSkel.c module, where they are documented. These include routines such as SkelWoa ("kill" the program) or SkelInit. Books such as *Inside Macintosh*, volumes 1–5, document all the routines in the Macintosh library.

A6. THE PARSER
A6.1 Overview

The parser for the system was developed using the Unix-based compiler development tools LEX and BISON. The purpose of the parser is to match an input sentence (a sequence of characters) against a set of grammar rules to determine if the sentence conforms to the grammar. If the sentence completely satisfies the grammar rules, a final acceptance status is returned. If the sentence partially satisfies the grammar rules but the rule requires additional text, a partial acceptance status is returned ("It's OK so far"). If the sentence is unacceptable, an error status is returned by the parser, along with a pointer to the incorrect text.

With the availability of the partial acceptance return status, the parser can be called by the engine whenever a button has been completely processed. Thus errors can be detected as they occur instead of at the end of the entire message.

The rest of this section discusses the development of the parser in the Unix environment and the steps required to migrate the parser into the system in the Macintosh environment.

A6.2 Parser Development

A6.2.1 LEX and BISON Compiler Development Tools.

The parser for the system was developed using tools available on any Unix system: LEX and BISON. LEX, the standard Unix lexical analysis program generator, uses a set of user-defined regular expression definitions to create a function *yylex()* that recognizes occurrences of those expressions (tokens) in an input sequence. BISON, the parser generator developed by the GNU Project at Massachusetts Institute of Technology (MIT), uses a set of user-defined context free grammar (CFG) rules to create a function *yyparse()* that determines whether an input sentence conforms to the rules. BISON was used as a replacement for the standard Unix parser generator YACC (Yet Another Compiler-Compiler). Bison is upwardly compatible with the input files designed for YACC, but BISON permits a much larger grammar to be implemented. This became an issue as the controller lexicon grew. In fact, LEX itself had to be modified slightly to accommodate the rather large set of regular expressions that make up the controller lexicon. This modified version of LEX was called MYLEX.

A6.2.2 Parser Code Structure.

The parser consists of two main functions: *yylex()* and *yyparse()*. The *yyparse()* function compares an input sentence against a set of context-free rules. It repeatedly calls the *yylex()* function whenever it needs the next token from the input sentence. The *yyparse()* function must be called by a *main()* function. In the Macintosh environment, this function is the engine, discussed above. However, to test the parser in the Unix environment, a very simple main program can be written. Such a function may be available in a YACC library, but it can be written very easily. One possible main function would be the following:

```
main()
{
    while(1)
        yyparse();
}
```

In addition to a main program, error functions *yyerror()* and *yywrap()* are required. The *yywrap()* function is provided in the standard LEX library. The *yyerror()* function may or may not be present. If not, it can be written very easily. The following simple *yyerror()* function has been used thus far, but a more complicated one could be written:

```
yyerror( errmsg ) char *errmsg;
{
      printf("%s\n", errmsg);
}
```

A6.2.3 Grammar Source Files. The lexicon is specified in two source files, one for LEX and the other for BISON. For the controller grammar, these files are called *atc.l* and *atc.y*, respectively. For the pilot grammar, they are called *pilot.l* and *pilot.y*. The LEX source file has the following sections.

program section:	C code to be included in the *yylex()* module
lexical analyzer table sizes:	
	Maximum number of nodes, positions, states, etc.
definitions:	Low-level definitions of expressions used in LEX rules
LEX rules section:	Series of regular expressions that make up tokens

The BISON source file has the following sections:

token definitions:	Definitions of tokens returned by the function *yylex()*
grammar rules:	Rules of the grammar in a BNF-like syntax, including actions to be taken when a rule is matched to an input sequence (generally *printf* statements)
program section:	Any C code to be included in the *yyparse()* module

The guiding principle used in the parser developed thus far has been to define the LEX basic units of the grammar that are used in multiple fragments unless these units are extremely complex. For example, *time* is defined as a token. On the other hand, although *fix* is used as a basic component throughout the phraseology, the definition of fix is much too complex to justify its definition as a token. Moreover, several of its subcomponents are used (as basic components in and of themselves) in other fragments. *Altitude* was originally defined as a token in LEX that could be returned by one of two rules, one for altitude and the other for flight level. The two rules were subsequently transferred to BISON, however, and the original token was split into two separate tokens (one for altitude and one for flight level) because altitude (in the narrow sense of the word) was explicitly used in the phraseology.

Items such as location names and facility names have been implemented as tokens for which the actual proper nouns are listed as separate LEX rules that return the appropriate tokens; for example, *Boston*, *Baltimore*, *Chicago*, *Atlanta*, and *Los Angeles* all return the token *LNAME*. The proper way to handle this is to define a marker, such as a percent sign, to prefix any proper name, and then have an action associated with the BISON rule containing the token that calls a subroutine to check a table (probably a balanced tree file) containing all the specific valid strings for that token.

Similarly, tokens that include numbers, such as *time* and *heading*, need to be screened for invalid numbers. This can be accomplished fairly easily by associating an action with each BISON rule that contains such a token. The action should call a subroutine that takes a literal to identify the token type and the value of the specific token instance. The subroutine could then do a simple table lookup and return a flag indicating whether the value is valid.

A6.2.4 Building the Parser. Perform the following steps: (1) Produce the lexical analyzer module by typing:

mylex atc.l (pilot.l for pilot grammar)

The file *lex.yy.c* will be generated, unless there are errors in the LEX source file. In particular, watch out for the grammar exceeding the limits defined in the table-size section of the LEX source file. LEX will generate statistics that show the current usage and limits of each parameter. If the lexical source exceeds a limit, simply increase that limit.

(2) Produce the parser module by typing:

bison -y -d -v atc.y

The file *y.tab.c* will be generated.

The -y option forces the parser file to be named using the YACC convention *y.tab.c*. Otherwise the parser file would be named based on the name of the BISON source file.

The -d option causes the file *y.tab.h* to be generated and is required for the build.

The -v option causes the file *y.output* to be generated. This file is not needed for the parser, but it is useful in debugging the grammar if there are any rule conflicts.

(3) Compile and link:

    cc parser.c lex.yy.c y.tab.c yyerror.c -ll -o dlink

The result of this command will be an executable file called *dlink*. The file *parser.c* is assumed to contain the *main()* function, and *yyerror.c* is assumed to contain the function *yyerror()*. The *-ll* option links with the LEX library, where the function *yywrap()* is found. The *-o dlink* option specifies that the executable file should be named *dlink*. Otherwise the executable file would have been called the default *a.out*.

BISON uses some constructs that are part of the new ANSI C standard. If a C compiler does not support ANSI C, it is likely that *y.tab.c* will not compile. We have encountered a problem with the *const* symbol used in parser table definitions. By globally removing all occurrences of *const* from *y.tab.c*, we have successfully gotten around the problem on one particular Unix system.

A6.2.5 Running/Testing the Parser.   To run the parser in the Unix environment, type the following:

    dlink

The behavior of the parser depends on the specific *main()* function being used. For the one suggested earlier, the parser waits for a message to be typed in terminated with the word *over* followed by a carriage return. At that point the *yyparse()* function is called; this will terminate if either: (1) an error is encountered or (2) the phrase *over* (with upper- or lowercase *O* and with or without a period) is entered. If the message parses successfully, an inverted parse tree will currently be written to the standard input device, consisting of the names of the parser grammar rules that were encountered in the input sentence. If an error is encountered—that is, an incorrect token is returned from *yylex()*—the standard error routine is called, which prints the token and message *parse error*.

If *yylex()* encounters input that does not match any rule, it simply prints that input to the standard output (the screen in this case) and continues processing the input until it recognizes a token, which it then returns to *yyparse()*. In other words, *yyparse()* is never made aware of the superfluous input, so a syntax error is not generated. This is not a problem in the Macintosh environment, where superfluous input would never be passed to the parser from the engine. However, with the stand-alone parser in the Unix environment, this could be handled in the manner suggested in the following paragraphs.

To force the generation of an error in such cases, a wild-card rule was added to the LEX input so that any string of alphanumeric characters not recognized by one of the other rules would return the token *AAGH*. Although this yielded the desired result, it had the unfortunate side effect of greatly limiting the number of rules that could be defined in the LEX input. The wild-card rule generates such a huge number of transitions in the deterministic finite automaton that it limits to an unacceptable degree the number of other rules that can be specified. Fortunately, a modified version of LEX, called MYLEX, solved this problem.

A6.3 Parser Enhancement

The original parser for an earlier version of the system has been enhanced so that it can return a partial success/failure status, given an incomplete input sentence. To accomplish this feature, a number of changes were made to the LEX and BISON source files and to the resulting parser files *lex.yy.c* and *y.tab.c*. The changes required to the parser files are generated automatically by two filter programs, discussed in detail in sections 6.4.3 and 6.4.4.

The required changes were as follows:

(1) LEX source file changes.

The following was inserted at the beginning of the LEX source file:

```
%{
#include "y.tab.h"
extern char in_sent[];
%}
```

The file *y.tab.h* is the file produced by BISON that assigns numerical values to the tokens returned by the lexical analyzer. The character string *in_sent* is used to redefine the input routines to get input from a string buffer instead of from the standard input device, *stdin*.

The following rule was added at the end of the LEX source file so that words not in the language cause an error token to be returned, instead of being ignored.

```
[^ \n\t]+                {return(AAGH);}
```

(2) BISON source file changes.

The following token definition was included near the top of the BISON source file:

%token AAGH

(3) Parser code changes to the file *y.tab.c*.
At the beginning of the file the following was inserted:

```
extern char out_sent[];
extern char yytext[];
```

The variable *out_sent* is a string returned by the parser and used by the mainline to determine if the sentence parsed was "OK so far." The variable *yytext* is a string returned by the lexical analyzer and contains the text corresponding to the last token seen.

In the middle of the file, immediately after the comment line /*Shift the lookahead token*/ the following was inserted:

```
strcat(out_sent,yytext);
strcat(out_sent," ");
```

Next, the routines in the parser responsible for recovery after an error were disabled. These routines were not wanted in the parser because we wanted it to fail as soon as an error was detected. All lines from the line immediately following label *yyerrlab:* to the line preceding the label *yyerrdefault:* were deleted, except for *yyabort;*. Immediately above the *yyabort* line, the following was added:

```
yysptr = yysbuf;
```

Next, all lines from the line containing the label *yyerrhandle:* (this label is not needed anymore) to the fifth line from the end of the file, immediately preceding the statement *yystate = yyn;* were deleted.

A6.4 Moving the Parser to the Macintosh Environment

Once the parser has been tested in the Unix environment, it can be moved into the THINK C version 4.0 environment on a Macintosh II computer. The required changes fall into two categories: LEX and BISON source file changes and *lex.yy.c* and *y.tab.c* parser code changes.

A6.4.1 Changes to the Grammar Source Files.
Make the following changes in the respective files: (1) In the LEX source file, make sure the following lines appear near the bottom of the file after a similar one for *over*.

```
"^"          {return (CARET);}
[^ \n\t]+    {return (AAGH);}
```

(2) In the BISON source file, first make sure the following lines appear as token definitions near the top of the file:

```
%token CARET
%token AAGH
```

Second, change the definition of *over* to be a simple phrase. Search for the rule that begins *phrase:*. This rule consists of a series of phrase definitions combined by *ors*. Add the lines:

```
| phrase OVER
    {pprintf("PHRASE\n");
    yyclearin;}
```

as the last part of the rule (but before the terminating semicolon).

Third, just below the previous change, change the rule *end : OVER;* to read:

```
end : CARET
    ;
```

Fourth, change all occurrences of *printf* to *pprintf*. The parser ordinarily prints out an inverted parse tree via the *printf* statements. This must not happen by default in the Macintosh version. Furthermore, *printf* defaults to the system console, a special window on the Macintosh. AIR needs to print to its own window; *pprintf()* is a routine in the engine that will do this.

Once the changes above have been made, the LEX and BISON source files can be processed. Type the following:

```
mylex atc.l        (pilot.l   for the pilot grammar)
bison -y -d atc.y
```

A6.4.2 Changes to the Parser.   Once the LEX and BISON source files have been changed and then rerun through LEX and BISON, as shown above, several changes are needed to make the parser fit into the Macintosh-based THINK C environment. Generally speaking, the changes fall into three categories: changes due to incompatibility between the BISON-generated parser and ANSI C; changes due to the parser enhancement (discussed previously) that allows partial success/failure status to be returned; and changes due to the data segment limits in the Macintosh environment. The changes are numerous and could not easily be made by hand each time a new version of the parser is developed. Therefore two utility "filter" programs were written that make all the changes automatically. These filters will be discussed in detail later.

The following are the changes due to BISON and ANSI C:

The *strpos.c* function had to be written and added to the system, since it was not part of the ANSI C library. Moreover, the BISON-generated parser contained two function calls that were not part of ANSI C. The Unix C function *alloca()* had to be replaced with calls to the ANSI function *malloc()*. The Unix C function *bcopy()* was written and made a part of the system; the function is the same as the ANSI C *strcpy()* function, but with the parameters reversed.

The changes due to the enhanced parser with partial success/failure status are discussed in section A6.3.

Instead of diving into the changes due to the data segment limitation of the Macintosh, some background discussion would be beneficial. Static memory is limited to 32K bytes in the Macintosh. That is, the data segment of the entire AIR System is limited to 32K bytes. In both the pilot and the controller parsers, *lex.yy.c* and *y.tab.c* initialize many large tables in static memory and overflow the data segment ceiling. This problem was solved by modifying the source code of both files to allocate the parsing tables dynamically. This is described in the THINK C manual and involves allocating memory from the heap. It was immediately realized that this process was too tedious to be performed manually by the programmer each time a new version of the parser was ready.

To automate the process of changing from static to dynamically allocated parser tables, two filter programs were written in the Unix environment. The first filter, called *LEXMAC*, reads the *lex.yy.c* function and generates a series of files that replace the original lexical analyzer. The second filter, called *BIGMAC*, performs a similar process for the file *y.tab.c*. Before discussing each of these filters individually, we can examine the general process of switching to dynamic memory allocation.

The basic idea is as follows. Instead of predefining an entire table of values, only a pointer to each table is declared statically. The C language treats pointers and array names as addresses, so both the fifth entry of an array *foo[]* and the fifth entry from the pointer **foo* are referred to as *foo[5]*. The C function *calloc()* is called once for each table, in order to accomplish the dynamic allocation. Next, each of the tables must be initialized with the corresponding values from the former preinitialization code. This is accomplished by the *LEXMAC* and *BIGMAC* filters in a two-step process. First, the data contained in the parser tables are removed from the parser files *lex.yy.c* and *y.tab.c* and written into new data files. Second, the filters generate the C code necessary to read the data from the new data files into the dynamically allocated tables.

A6.4.3 *LEXMAC* Filter.

The *LEXMAC* filter (LEX to Macintosh filter program) was written to automate the changes required to the lexical analyzer function *lex.yy.c* in order to prepare it for the Macintosh THINK C environment. In addition to the previously discussed static to dynamic allocation of parsing tables, other changes that previously were handled manually were also included in the filter. The resulting files that make up the parser can then be transferred to the Macintosh environment and included in the system.

LEXMAC consists of a regular expression file *lexmac.lxi* and a parser file *lexmac.c*. The regular expression file is actually a LEX source file, which is used to generate a *LEXMAC lex.yy.c* file that recognizes specific expressions in the AIR controller lexical analyzer file (also *lex.yy.c*, unfortunately). The file *lexmac.c* contains a main function that calls the *LEXMAC lex.yy.c* file (not to be confused with the AIR *lex.yy.c* file) to search the AIR *lex.yy.c* file for static tables and other items that must be altered.

The filter program can be modified as follows. First, the regular expression and parser files are modified to include whatever new filtering is required. Second, the regular expression file is run through LEX. Finally, the *lexmac.c* file is compiled and linked with the LEX library.

> lex lexmac.lxi
> cc lexmac.c -ll -o lexmac

To prepare the AIR *lex.yy.c* for the Macintosh environment, it must be run through the *LEXMAC* filter program as follows:

> lexmac < lex.yy.c

The lexical analyzer file is replaced by the following files:

lex.yy.lm.c	modified LEX-generated yylex()
y.tab.h	token definitions included in yylex() function module
lex.def.h	pointer definitions of lexical analysis tables
lex.alloc.c	dynamic allocation of lexical analysis tables
yyvstop.dat	data file for initialization of yyvstop[] table

yycrank.dat   data file for initialization of yycrank[] table
yysvec.dat   data file for initialization of yysvec[] table

The resulting AIR lexical analysis files should then be transferred to the Macintosh environment using Kermit or some other communications software.

Just for completeness, changes implemented by *LEXMAC* that are not related to the dynamic allocation of tables in memory are as follows:

(1) Redundant definition that must be removed:

#define NLSTATE yyprevious=YYNEWLINE

(2) The following two macro definitions are removed from *lex.yy.lm.c*:

```
#define output(c) putc(c,yyout)
#define input()
(((yytchar=yysptr>yysbuf?U(*--yysptr):getc(yyin))
   ==10?(yylineno++,yytchar):yytchar==EOF?0:yytchar)
```

(3) Make sure that *lex.h* is included in *lex.yy.lm.c*. This should have been part of the *atc.l* source file.

#include "lex.h"

A6.4.4 *BIGMAC* Filter.

The *BIGMAC* filter program (Bison Goes to MACintosh) was written to automate the changes required to the parser *y.tab.c* in order to prepare it for the Macintosh THINK C environment. In addition to the previously discussed static to dynamic allocation of parsing tables, other changes that were previously handled manually were also included in the filter. The resulting files that make up the parser can then be transferred to the Macintosh environment and included in the system.

BIGMAC consists of a regular expression file *bigmac.lxi* and a main program *bigmac.c*. The regular expression file is actually a LEX source file, which is used to generate a *BIGMAC lex.yy.c* file that recognizes specific expressions in the AIR controller parser file *y.tab.c*. The file *bigmac.c* contains a main function that calls the *BIGMAC lex.yy.c* file (not to be confused with the AIR *lex.yy.c* file) to search the AIR parser file *y.tab.c* for static tables and other items that must be altered.

The filter program can be modified as follows. First, the regular expression and *BIGMAC* main program are modified to include whatever new filtering is required. Second, the regular expression file is

run through LEX. Finally, the *BIGMAC* program is compiled and
linked with the LEX library.

    lex bigmac.lxi
    cc bigmac.c -ll -o bigmac

To prepare the AIR *y.tab.c* for the Macintosh environment, it must
be run through the *BIGMAC* filter program as follows:

    bigmac < y.tab.c

The parser file y.tab.c is replaced by the following files:

y.tab.bm.c	modified BISON-generated yyparse()
y.def.bm.h	parser table pointer definitions
y.alloc.bm.c	parser table dynamic allocation
y.init1.bm.c	first part of parser table initialization
y.int2.bm.c	second part of parser table initialization

A6.4.5 Transferring Parser Files to Macintosh.   Once the *LEX-
MAC* and *BIGMAC* filters have been run, the parser files can be transferred to the Macintosh using Kermit or some other communications
software. These files can be placed into the folder containing the system, replacing previous versions of the parser.

A6.5 Summary

The following is a step-by-step summary for modifying the parser:
    (1) Modify the LEX and BISON source files, as desired.
    (2) Run the LEX source file through LEX:

    mylex atc.y

(3) Run the BISON source file through BISON:

    bison -y -d atc.y

(4) Compile the parser in Unix:

    cc parser.c lex.yy.c y.tab.c yyerror.c -ll -o dlink

(5) Try running the parser:

    dlink

(6) When ready, edit the LEX and BISON source files and make sure
all the grammar source file changes outlined in section A6.4.1 have
been made.

(7) Run the lexical analyzer through the *LEXMAC* filter:

LEXMAC < lex.yy.c

(8) Run the parser through the *BIGMAC* filter:

BIGMAC < y.tab.c

(9) Transfer all of the parser files into the AIR System folder on the Macintosh.

A7. THE RESOURCE FILE
A7.1 Modifying an Existing Resource

ResEdit is a utility used to modify a resource file. The resource file is accessed by the engine portion of the system in order to display menus/icons/alerts. Since the information in a resource file is nearly transparent to the engine, the appearance and information content of one or more menus (AIR menus = collection of icons and text buttons) can be altered without changes or recompilation to the project.

Double clicking on ResEdit will start the editor; a list of disks/folders will be displayed. Keep double clicking folders until you reach the folder that contains the resource you want to edit. In some instances you may want to alter only the executable program (e.g., *demo*). Alterations to the executable code affect only that program; future versions built from the project file will not contain your changes. Alterations to the project resource file (which is incorporated into each application built by the project software) will be put into each application (such as *demo*). The project resource file is currently named *datalink.proj.rsrc*, although this name could be changed in the future.

Once an application or resource file has been double clicked, you will be presented with a list of resource categories (e.g., DLOG, ICON, DATA, ALRT). ICONs and DLOGs are most commonly used by the AIR software. To change an ICON, double click on *ICON* in the list and then double click the "replica" of the ICON you wish to alter. This will bring up the icon in a MacPaint-type *fat bits* editor (an enlarged 32 × 32 grid). Toggle the squares (bits) you wish to turn on/off by clicking on them with the mouse. You can save the results by clicking the *close* box of each window until you get an alert box that asks, "Save 'filename' before closing?" Answer yes. You may then *quit* (pull-down menu for *file*). The changes you made will appear in the application that you edited when the application is run. If you edited a project resource file, the changes will appear in the next application you build or when you choose *run* in one of the project pull-down menus.

A DLOG (dialogue) may be edited in a similar way. Double click DLOG, then double click the appropriate DLOG ID. The window will contain a miniature replica of the menu displayed by the system (e.g, a menu for *chk speed*). Double clicking on the replica will expand it to a full-sized menu displayed in a window (all windows in ResEdit are dragable). Button entries can be selected by clicking them once. They can be dragged or resized. Double clicking a button will open it so that the text it contains can be altered. To get rid of a button, select it and then choose *cut* from the *edit* pull-down menu. To create a new button, choose *new* from the *file* menu. This will result in a window with some selections to make. *Button* is the default choice (there are other types of controls that the AIR System typically does not use). The button is "enabled" by default. This means that when you click it (i.e., run the application), an "event" will happen. Keep it that way; otherwise the button will be dead. There will be an editable text box. Change the text from *new* to the word or phrase you wish for the button. The air traffic grammar is case sensitive, so use appropriate upper- or lowercase. Once you have made all your changes (to one or more DLOGS), close up in the same way described for the ICONs above.

A7.2 Adding a New Resource

New menus and their icons can be added to the file *datalink.proj.rsrc*. To add an icon, proceed as above until the window with the icon replicas is open. Choose *new* from the *file* pull-down menu. The same fat bits editor will be activated; create the icon you need. The new icon must have an ID that will correspond to the menu (DLOG) it is being created for. The following system is used. We add 10,000 to the ID of the DLOG to yield the icon ID. When the icon is double clicked by a user we subtract 10,000 to determine which menu (DLOG) to display. By convention level-one (main menu) DLOGs (menus) have IDs between 1,000 and 1,999; level-two (submenus) between 2,000 and 2,999, and so on. When creating an icon you should have already determined the next available DLOG ID that will correspond to the icon. The following process is used to give an icon a specific ID (by default, all new resources are given a "random" nonconflicting ID that can be changed to another unique number by the ResEdit user):

> With the current ICON open or selected choose *get info* from the *file* pull-down menu. Change the ID number to the one you want (corresponding DLOG ID + 10,000).

To create a new DLOG, proceed as you would have in editing an existing DLOG but choose *new* from the *file* pull-down menu once the list of DLOGs is displayed. A window with the new menu will be displayed. The window will display the DLOG ID in its title/drag bar. You will need to size the new menu (displayed in miniature as an "inner" window). Click on the forenamed title/drag bar of the "outer" window. Then use the *display as text* from the DLOG pull-down menu (top menu bar—rightmost) to open an information box. The window coordinates can be entered in the appropriate box; they should match those for the "main menu." You can also add a title. The same box also will receive the ResID for the DLOG; this is explained below. Double click (open) the "inner" window (the menu being created) and create buttons and text as above. Once you have the menu the way you want it, you can change the ID to be the appropriate one as follows:

> With the DLOG opened or selected, choose *get info* from the *file* pulldown menu. Change the ID to the appropriate one.
>
> With the DLOG opened, click on its title/drag bar. Choose *display as text* from the pull-down menu called DLOG. Change the ResID to the DLOG ID number you used in the last step.
>
> Double click the "menu" you have created within the DLOG window. Choose *get info* from the *file* pull-down menu. Change the DITL ID to be the same as the DLOG ID.

Sometimes a new icon or DLOG will not show up in a list until the ICON or DLOG list is closed and reopened. It will also be necessary to add appropriate defines and DialogPtrs to the *datalink.c* program.

A7.3 Text to Display on a Button

Each button has a size (determined by top, left, bottom, and right) and a single text item that can be edited with ResEdit. The text will always be displayed centered within the button, with the text that does not fit within the button invisible to the user. Thus, if the text were:

"I can see nothing plain"

and the button were large enough to hold the entire string, it would all appear within the button. If the button could hold only nineteen of the twenty-three characters, however, the following would be displayed in the button:

can see nothing pla

If you want only the first three words to appear, size the button for nine or ten characters and place enough blanks in the front of the text to balance the "nothing plain" at the end of the text, thus:

"   I can see nothing plain"

The button would appear as:

   I can see

but the entire text would be sent to the engine whenever the button was hit.

A7.4 Processing of the Text from a Button by the AIR System Engine

The text is processed as follows:

(1) The text is scanned from left to right;

(2) Consecutive multiple blanks are converted to a single blank;

(3) The string is first divided into three parts to discard the first comment. The second (comment) part is that text between the first occurrence from the left of a * followed by any text followed by the first occurrence of a $. The first part is the text before the occurrence of the * and the third part is the text after the $. Any of these parts may be null. The second part, including the * and the $, is treated as a comment and discarded. The first part and third part are concatenated together. If there are no * and $, then the entire string will be treated as a first part.

An example of the use of comments would be the following:

   "*(MHz) $<DONE>"
   _ = = = = =_ _ _ _ _ _

where, because of the blanks and the size of the button as shown by the underlining, only (*MHz*) is displayed on the button (as an alternative for the user to entering *kHz*, which appears on another button). Yet the action of the (MHz) button is to signal the completion of the input from the dialogue and not to enter the MHz into the output string, since MHz is not expected by the parser.

(4) The string is again divided into three parts, this time searching for the text between the first occurrence from the left of a < and then a >. The text to the left of the first < is also added to the output string, the text between the first < and the > then brings up a bracketed dialogue, and the text after the > then is saved to be processed after the bracketed dialogue is completed. When this third string of text is pro-

cessed, it is treated just as if it had been entered via a button selection; that is, it is scanned from left to right, multiple blanks are replaced with a single one, it is divided into three parts for comment, and so on.

An example of the recursive nature of the text scanning would be a button that was sized to display about eight characters with a text of:

" from <lname> <fix>"
———— = = = = =————

Only <*lname*> would appear on the button, as shown by the underlining. The effect of hitting the button is as follows:

(a) to add the text "from," with a blank in front and back, to the output string;

(b) to bring up a <lname> bracketed dialogue;

(c) when the user had finished entering into the <lname> dialogue, a <fix> bracketed dialogue would be automatically brought up.

A8. The Grammar
A8.1 Syntax for Grammar Definition

The syntax used in the grammar specification given below in section A8.2 is as follows:

- All uppercase letters indicate that the words are to be spoken verbatim.
- All lowercase letters enclosed in angle brackets indicate *tokens*, that is, variables whose syntax has been previously defined.
- Text in italics followed by a colon is used to specify conditions for alternative phrases.
- Brackets indicate that the enclosed data may or may not be applicable.
- Braces indicate that the enclosed data represent a description of what is to be said.
- Parentheses are used for grouping or to set off explanatory text (indicated by italics).
- A slash indicates that one of the two words the slash separates is to be selected.
- A vertical line, generally used in conjunction with parentheses, indicates that one of the two groups of words the vertical line separates is to be selected.
- An ampersand indicates that both words or phrases separated by the ampersand are to be used.
- When alternatives are provided for entire sentences, they are separated by an *or* indented on one line.

- A double plus sign indicates one or more repetitions of the preceding token; a plus sign followed by a number indicates that the preceding token should be repeated for a total of times equal to the given number.

Example
MAINTAIN/CRUISE <altitude>.
   or
MAINTAIN <altitude> (UNTIL <time> | PAST <fix> | <digit++>) MILES/MINUTES PAST <fix>).
   where altitude has been previously defined as:
If the number of feet is less than 18,000:
   ALTITUDE <digit++> THOUSAND [<digit> HUNDRED]
else:
   FLIGHT LEVEL <digit++>
where digit, time, and fix have also been previously defined.

A8.2 AIR System Controller Grammar

The current grammar for the protocol language of the controller interface is as follows:

Token Definitions

<ffunction>	(facility function)
	Note: may not include all possible values
<lname>	(location name)
	Note: currently includes only a few cities
<clock-az>	<digit++> O'CLOCK
<direction>	<quad> | <location>
<quad>	NORTH | SOUTH | EAST | WEST
<location>	NORTHEAST | NORTHWEST | SOUTHEAST | SOUTHWEST
<miles>	<digit++> MILES
<rel-movement>	CLOSING | CONVERGING | PARALLEL | OPPOSITE | DIVERGING | OVERTAKING | CROSSING (LEFT TO RIGHT | RIGHT TO LEFT)
<bird-species>	DUCKS/GEESE/GULLS/SPARROWS
<bird-size>	SMALL/LARGE
<digit>	0/1/2/3/4/5/6/7/8/9
<ltime>	(local time indicator)
	Note: currently includes only EST/MT/PST
<time>	<digit++> (<ltime> | ZULU)
	Note: <time> was simplified to make the interface dialogue easier to understand.

\<altimeter\>	ALTIMETER IS \<digit++\>
\<heading\>	HEADING \<digit++\>
\<frequency\>	\<digit++\> [(.\<digit\> [\<digit\>] | KHZ)]
\<speed\>	\<digit++\> KNOTS
\<mach number\>	MACH [1]. \<digit\> [\<digit\>]
\<altitude\>	*If the number of feet is less than 18,000:*
	ALTITUDE \<digit++\> THOUSAND
	[\<digit\> HUNDRED]
	else:
	FLIGHT LEVEL \<digit++\>
\<fname\>	(facility name)
	Note: currently includes only a few; for example, Logan
\<craft-type\>	(type of aircraft)
	Note: currently only DC-8 and APACHE defined
\<route\>	VICTOR \<digit++\> [ROMEO | \<location\>],
	or
	J \<digit++\> [ROMEO],
	\<LMF-color\> \<digit++\>,
	or
	NORTH AMERICAN ROUTE \<digit++\>,
	or
	(IR | VR) \<digit++\>.
\<LMF-color\>	(color of L/MF airway)
	Note: currently only RED/BLUE
\<navaid\>	VOR/VOR-TAC/TACAN/RADIO BEACON
\<fix\>	(\<lname\> \<navaid\> | \<lname\> (DME FIX | WAYPOINT | \<radial\> | \<localizer\> | \<fix-azimuth\>))
	Note: definitions for radial, localizer, and fix-azimuth have not yet been provided, as there are too many unknowns
\<weather-level\>	(LEVEL 1 WEAK | LEVEL 2 MODERATE | LEVEL 3 INTENSE | LEVEL 4 | LEVEL 5 | LEVEL 6 EXTREME)

Legal Phrases in ATC Grammar

LOW ALTITUDE ALERT. CHECK YOUR ALTITUDE IMMEDIATELY. THE (((MEAM\|MVA\|MOCA\|MIA) IN YOUR AREA) \| MDA \| DH) IS \<altitude\>.

TRAFFIC ALERT [\<clock-az\>\|\<direction\>, \<miles\>, [\<quad\>BOUND], \<rel-movement\>]. ADVISE YOU [TURN

LEFT/RIGHT [<heading>] AND] CLIMB/DESCEND [TO <altitude>]
IMMEDIATELY.

CONTACT (<fname>|<lname>) <ffunction> [<frequency>] [AT
(<time>|<fix>|<altitude)].

CHANGE TO MY FREQUENCY <frequency>.

REMAIN THIS FREQUENCY.

TRAFFIC, <clock-az>|<direction>, <miles>, [<quad>BOUND],
<rel-movement>, [<craft-type>,] (<altitude> | ALTITUDE
UNKNOWN).

[<clock-az> | <direction>] TRAFFIC NO LONGER A FACTOR.

TRAFFIC, (<miles> | <digit++> MINUTES) <direction> OF
(<fname|<fix>), <direction>BOUND, [<craft-type>,]
(<altitude> | ALTITUDE UNKNOWN). ESTIMATED <fix> <time>,
or

TRAFFIC, NUMEROUS TARGETS VICINITY (<fname>|<fix>).

FLOCK OF (<bird-species> | [<bird-size>] BIRDS), <direction>BOUND
ALONG <route> | <clock-az> <miles> <direction>BOUND |
VICINITY (<fname>|<fix>)), (LAST REPORTED AT <altitude> |
ALTITUDE UNKNOWN),
or

NUMEROUS FLOCKS (<bird-species> | [<bird-size>] BIRDS),
VICINITY (<fname>|<fix>), (LAST REPORTED AT <altitude> |
ALTITUDE UNKNOWN).

REQUEST FLIGHT CONDITIONS [OVER <fix> | ALONG PRESENT ROUTE |
BETWEEN <fix> AND <fix>].

(WEATHER/CHAFF) AREA BETWEEN <clock-az> AND <clock-az>
<miles>.
or

<digit++> MILE BAND OF (WEATHER/CHAFF) FROM [<miles>
<direction> OF] <fix> TO [<miles> <direction> OF] <fix>.
or

<weather-level> WEATHER ECHO BETWEEN <clock-az> AND
<clock-az> <miles>, MOVING <direction> AT <digit++>
KNOTS TOPS <altitude>.
or

DEVIATION APPROVED. ADVISE WHEN ABLE TO (RETURN TO COURSE
| RESUME NORMAL NAVIGATION).
or

UNABLE DEVIATION. (FLY <heading> | PROCEED DIRECT TO
<fix>).

Note: Deviation fragments are made more clear here. Official
manual is ambiguous on this point.

HOLD (SHORT OF RUNAWAY) | (IN POSITION).

Note: Terminal control messages are not part of current
interface.

WIND SHEAR (ALERT) | (ALERTS (TWO | SEVERAL | ALL) QUADRANTS).
CENTERFIELD WIND <direction> AT <speed> (, <direction>
BOUNDARY WIND <direction> AT <speed>) | (VARYING TO
<direction> AT <speed>).

CLEARED to <fix> VIA ((<route>|<fix>)++).
Note: This message was used to group together all messages
starting with *VIA* or involving route assignment.

CLEARED TO FLY <direction> OF <lname> <Navaid Type> BETWEEN
THE <number> AND THE <number> (COURSES TO | BEARINGS
FROM | RADIALS) WITHIN <number> MILE RADIUS.
or
CLEARED TO FLY <quadrant> QUADRANT OF <lname> <Navaid
Type> WITHIN <number> MILE RADIUS.
or
CLEARED TO FLY <direction> OF THE <lname> M-L-S RUNWAY
<runway-num> BETWEEN THE <number> AND THE
<number> AZIMUTHS WITHIN/BETWEEN <number> MILE
RADIUS.

CLEARED DIRECT TO THE <fix> [, OFFSET <miles> RIGHT/LEFT OF
<route>].
Note: CLEARED was added, and the fragment *OFFSET* was added to
the fragment *DIRECT*. The *DIRECT* fragment was generalized to
contain all valid fixes.

MAINTAIN/CRUISE ALTITUDE [UNTIL (<time> | PAST <fix> | <miles>
PAST <fix> | <digit++> MINUTES PAST <fix>)].

[CLIMB/DESCEND AND] MAINTAIN <altitude> [(AFTER PASSING <fix>)
| (AT <time>) | (WHEN ESTABLISHED AT LEAST (<miles> |
<digit++> MINUTES) PAST <fix>)].
or
CLIMB/DESCEND TO REACH <altitude> [AT (<time> | <fix>)].
Note: AT <TIME>|<FIX> made optional in *CLIMB TO REACH*
message.

CROSS <fix> AT ((OR ABOVE/BELOW <altitude>) | (AND MAINTAIN
<altitude>)).
Note: The phrase above allows all possible combinations of
<altitude> requirements in a *CROSS* <FIX> phrase.

CLIMB/DESCEND AT PILOT'S DISCRETION.
Note: AT PILOT'S DISCRETION was implemented as an option.

MAINTAIN <altitude> THROUGH <altitude>.
Note: Referred to as <block altitude>.

EXPECT CLIMB/DESCENT CLEARANCE (IN <miles> | IN <number>
MINUTES | AT <fix>).

REQUEST ALTITUDE CHANGE FROM <fname> [AT
(<time>|<fix>|<altitude>)].

EXPECT FURTHER CLEARANCE VIA ((<fix>|<route>)++).

Note: (routing) was assumed to refer to any combination of routes and fixes used to describe a clearance.

CLEARED TO <fix>, HOLD <direction>, AS PUBLISHED.

or

CLEARED TO <fix>, NO DELAY EXPECTED.

EXPECT FURTHER CLEARANCE AT (<time>|<fix>) [ANTICIPATE ADDITIONAL <number> (MINUTE/HOUR) (DELAY AT <fix> | EN ROUTE DELAY | TERMINAL DELAY)].

Note: (time) was changed to *AT <TIME>|<FIX>.*

DELAY INDEFINITE, EXPECT FURTHER CLEARANCE <time>.

Note: DELAY INDEFINITE was made an optional preface to all *EXPECT* messages.

CLEARED TO <fix> VIA LAST ROUTING CLEARED.

CLEARED TO <fix>, HOLD <direction> OF <fix> ON THE (<number> RADIAL | <number> COURSE | <number> BEARING | <number> AZIMUTH |<route>) [, <number> MILE LEGS] [, LEFT/RIGHT TURNS].

PRIMARY RADAR OUT OF SERVICE. TRAFFIC ADVISORIES AVAILABLE ON TRANSPONDER AIRCRAFT ONLY.

| SHOW YOUR POSITION AS (PASSING <fix> | <miles> FROM <fix> | <miles> <direction> OF (<fix>|<lname>) | CROSSING/JOINING/DEPARTING <route> | INTERCEPTING/CROSSING <lname> <number> RADIAL).

Note: OVER/PASSING <FIX> was changed to *PASSING <FIX>* to avoid confusion with *OVER* that is used in parser to signify end of message (transmit). Also, note that | SHOW YOUR POSITION AS was added as a preface to make these into controller messages, where usually they are pilot responses to controller queries.

RADAR SERVICE TERMINATED.

SQUAWK MAYDAY ON 7700.

RADAR CONTACT <fix>. IF FEASIBLE, SQUAWK <code>.

Note: <fix> was used above instead of *(position).*

SQUAWK STANDBY.

RESET TRANSPONDER, SQUAWK <code>.

YOUR TRANSPONDER APPEARS INOPERATIVE, RESET, SQUAWK <code>.

Note: manual shows *INOPERATIVE/MALFUNCTIONING*

SAY ALTITUDE.

VERIFY ALTITUDE AND ALTIMETER SETTING.

STOP ALTITUDE SQUAWK. ALTITUDE DIFFERS BY <DIGIT++> FEET.

VERIFY AT <altitude>.

or

VERIFY ASSIGNED ALTITUDE <altitude>.

AFFIRMATIVE <altitude>.

or

NEGATIVE. [CLIMB/DESCEND AND] MAINTAIN <altitude>.
Note: This phraseology was omitted from interface, because it requires a pilot-initiated dialogue, which has not yet been addressed. Also, *AFFIRMATIVE/NEGATIVE* could apply to any controller response to pilot-initiated queries.

SQUAWK ALTITUDE.
> *or*
> STOP ALTITUDE SQUAWK.

STOP SQUAWK.

SQUAWK <code> [AND IDENT].

SQUAWK STANDBY.
> *then,*
> SQUAWK <code>.

RADAR CONTACT [<fix>].
> *Note:* <fix> was used above instead of *(position)*.

RADAR CONTACT LOST.
> *Note:* syntax for *(alternative instructions when required)* was not known, so it was omitted in the grammar fragment above.

TURN LEFT/RIGHT <heading>.
> *or*
> FLY <heading>.
> *or*
> FLY PRESENT HEADING.
> *or*
> DEPART <fix> <heading>.
> *Note:* FLY *<heading>* and FLY PRESENT HEADING were implemented as a choice at the end of a *VECTOR* phraseology.

TURN <degrees> DEGREES LEFT/RIGHT.

THIS WILL BE A NO-GYRO VECTOR, TURN LEFT/RIGHT.
> *or*
> STOP TURN.

FOR VECTOR TO (<fix>|<airway>).
> *or*
> FOR VECTOR TO INTERCEPT <lname> <number> RADIAL.
> *or*
> VECTOR FOR SPACING.
> *or*
> FOR VECTOR TO <lname> FINAL APPROACH COURSE.

RESUME OWN NAVIGATION.
> *or*
> FLY <heading>. WHEN ABLE, PROCEED DIRECT <fix>.
> *Note: (position with respect to course/fix)* removed from RESUME
> OWN NAVIGATION. Also, WHEN ABLE . . . removed from FLY
> *<HEADING>*—it is implemented as part of *DEVIATION* messages.

(ACCELERATE | [IF PRACTICAL,] SLOW) TO (SPEED <speed> | (<mach-number>)

> *or*

(INCREASE | [IF PRACTICAL,] REDUCE SPEED BY (<number> KNOTS | <mach-number>).

> *Note:* Confusion among homonyms eliminated by revision.

SAY AIRSPEED.

> *or*

MAINTAIN PRESENT SPEED.

> *or*

DO NOT EXCEED <speed>.

> *Note:* IF PRACTICAL, was added as an optional preface.

(SLOW TO (SPEED <speed> | <mach number>) | REDUCE SPEED BY (<number> KNOTS | <mach number>)). THEN, DESCEND AND MAINTAIN <altitude>.

> *or*

DESCEND AND MAINTAIN <altitude>. THEN, (SLOW TO (SPEED <speed> | <mach number>) | REDUCE SPEED BY (<number> KNOTS | <mach number>)).

CROSS <fix> AT (OR ABOVE/BELOW <altitude> | AND MAINTAIN (<altitude>|<block altitude>)) AT <speed>.

> *Note:* The phrase above allows for all possible combinations of <speed> and <altitude> requirements for a CROSS <FIX> phrase.

RESUME NORMAL SPEED.

Notes

PREFACE

1. Julien Offroy de La Mettrie, *Man the Machine*, annotated by Gertrude Carman Bussey (La Salle, Ill.: Open Court, 1912). Quoted in John Aach, "Science and Commonsense Skepticism," *Skeptical Inquirer* 16 (Fall 1991): 51–57.

INTRODUCTION

1. Steven Cushing, *Language and Communication-Related Problems of Aviation Safety,* ERIC Document Reproduction Service ED 296 595, FL 017 504. (Washington, D.C.: U.S. Department of Education, 1988); idem, "Social/Cognitive Mismatch as a Source of Fatal Language Errors: Implications for Standardization," in *Proceedings, Fourth International Aviation English Forum: Aviation English Standards* (Paris, 1991); idem, "Social/Cognitive Mismatch as a Source of Fatal Language Errors," in *Proceedings, Fifteenth International Congress of Linguists* (Quebec, 1992).

2. Steven Cushing, "From Where They Look to What They Think: Determining Controllers' Cognitive Strategies from Oculometer Scanning Data," in *NASA Contractor Report 181894,* comp. Surendra N. Tiwari, contract NGT 47-003-029, NASA-Langley Research Center, Hampton, Virginia (Springfield, Va.: National Technical Information Service, 1989); idem, Letter, *The Sciences* 30 (January–February 1990): 14; idem, "The Cognitive Space of Air Traffic Control: A Parametric Dynamic Topological Model," in *Proceedings, Twelfth Annual Conference of the Cognitive Science Society* (Cambridge: Massachusetts Institute of Technology, 1990).

3. Steven Cushing, Suzanne Artemieff, Gabriel Elkin, Barry Paine, Susan Willard, Ann Sisco, and David Ross, *An Error-Resistant Linguistic Protocol for Air Traffic Control,* Final Report, contract NAG 2-564, NASA-Ames Research Center, (Mountain View, Calif., 1989); Steven Cushing, "'Air Cal Three Thirty Six, Go around Three Thirty Six, Go Around': Linguistic Repetition in Air/Ground Communication," in

Barbara Johnstone, ed., *Repetition in Discourse: Interdisciplinary Perspectives* (Norwood, N.J.: Ablex, 1994).

4. Spanish Ministry of Transport and Communications, "Spaniards Analyze Tenerife Accident," trans. U.S. National Transportation Safety Board, *Aviation Week and Space Technology* 109 (20 November 1978): 113–21; Spanish Ministry of Transport and Communications, "Clearances Cited in Tenerife Collision," trans. U.S. National Transportation Safety Board, *Aviation Week and Space Technology* (27 November 1978): 67–74.

5. National Transportation Safety Board, "Aircraft Accident Report: Air California Flight 336 Boeing 737-293, N468AC, John Wayne Orange County Airport, Santa Ana, California, February 17, 1981," report NTSB-AAR-81-12, 1981.

6. National Transportation Safety Board, "Aircraft Accident Report: Eastern Airlines, Inc., L-1011, N310EA, Miami, Florida, December 29, 1972," report NTSB-AAR-73-14, 1973.

7. Associated Press, "Avianca Tape Shows Confusion in Cockpit," *Boston Globe*, 28 March 1990.

8. For example, Noam Chomsky has postulated the existence of an inborn system of grammatical "parameters that have to be fixed by experience" as children go about learning their first language; *Lectures on Government and Binding* (Dordrecht: Foris, 1981), p. 4. See also Steven Cushing, *The Formal Semantics of Quantification* (Ann Arbor, Mich.: University Microfilms, 1976); idem, *Quantifier Meanings: A Study in the Dimensions of Semantic Competence*, North-Holland Linguistic Series, vol. 48 (Amsterdam: North-Holland, 1982); idem, "Dynamic Model Selection in the Interpretation of Discourse," in *Cognitive Constraints on Communication: Representations and Processes*, ed. L. Vaina and J. Hintikka (Dordrecht: Reidel, 1984); idem, Letter, *The Sciences* 30 (January–February 1990): 14; idem, "Prototypical Considerations on Modal Meanings," in *Meanings and Prototypes: Studies on Linguistic Categorization*, ed. S. L. Tsohatzidis (New York: Routledge, 1990); idem, Review of S. N. Sridhar, *Cognition and Sentence Production: A Crosslinguistic Study, Journal of Cross-Cultural Psychology* 21 (1990): 404–6; idem, "Explaining a Missing Modal Meaning: Ideology and Paradigm as Pragmatic Parameter," in *Levels of Linguistic Adaptation: Selected Papers from the 1987 International Pragmatics Conference*, ed. J. Verschueren (Philadelphia: Benjamins, 1991).

9. Cushing, *Quantifier Meanings;* idem, "Two Explanatory Principles in Semantics," in *Matters of Intelligence*, ed. L. Vaina (Dordrecht: Reidel, 1987); idem, "Cognitive Space of Air Traffic Control"; idem, "Prototypical Considerations on Modal Meanings."

10. Cushing, "Social/Cognitive Mismatch as a Source of Fatal Lan-

guage Errors" (1991); idem, "Social/Cognitive Mismatch as a Source of Fatal Language Errors" (1992).

11. See the following for related background work: C. E. Billings and E. S. Cheaney, eds., *Information Transfer Problems in the Aviation System*, NASA Technical Paper 1875 (Springfield, Va.: National Technical Information Service, 1981); G. W. Flathers II, *Development of an Air Ground Data Exchange Concept: Flight Deck Perspective*, NASA Contractor Report 4074, contract NAS1-17974, NASA-Langley Research Center, Hampton, Va. (Springfield, Va.: National Technical Information Service, 1987); Charlotte Linde, "Who's in Charge Here? Cooperative Work and Authority Negotiation in Police Helicopter Missions," in *Proceedings, Second Annual ACM Conference on Computer Supported Collaborative Work* (1988); idem, "The Quantitative Study of Communicative Success: Politeness and Accidents in Aviation Discourse," *Language in Society* 17, no. 3 (1988): 375–99; Jeremy Mell, "English Language Requirements of OCCAs (Air Traffic Controllers) in France and Training Problems," unpublished report. Université de Toulouse II (le Mirail), Section des Sciences du Langage, 1987.

12. National Transportation Safety Board, "Aircraft Accident Report: Allegheny Airlines, Inc., BAC 1-11, N1550, Rochester, New York, July 9, 1978," report NTSB-AAR-79-2, 1979.

13. National Transportation Safety Board, "Aircraft Accident Report: United Airlines, Inc., McDonnell-Douglas DC-8-61, N8082U, Portland, Oregon, December 28, 1978," report NTSB-AAR-79-7, 1979.

Chapter One

1. Noam Chomsky, "A Transformational Approach to Syntax," in *Proceedings of the Third Texas Conference on Problems of Linguistic Analysis in English, 1958*, ed. A. A. Hill (Austin: University of Texas, 1962).

2. *Callback*, no. 49 (July 1983).

3. *Callback*, no. 61 (July 1984).

4. *Callback*, no. 66 (December 1984).

5. *Callback*, no. 75 (September 1985).

6. *Callback*, no. 104 (February 1988).

7. Spanish Ministry of Transport and Communications, "Spaniards Analyze Tenerife Accident," trans. U.S. National Transportation Safety Board, *Aviation Week and Space Technology* 109 (20 November 1978): 113–21; idem, "Clearances Cited in Tenerife Collision," trans. U.S. National Transportation Safety Board, *Aviation Week and Space Technology* 109 (27 November 1978): 67–74.

8. National Transportation Safety Board, "Aircraft Accident Report: Air California Flight 336 Boeing 737-293, N468AC, John Wayne Orange County Airport, Santa Ana, California, February 17, 1981," report NTSB-AAR-81-12, 1981.

9. *Callback,* no. 9 (March 1980).
10. *Callback,* no. 58 (April 1984).
11. *Callback,* no. 75 (September 1985).
12. *Callback,* no. 19 (January 1981).
13. *Callback,* no. 7 (January 1980).
14. *Callback,* no. 61 (July 1984).
15. *Callback,* no. 22 (April 1981).
16. *Callback,* no. 88 (October 1986).
17. *Callback,* no. 149 (October 1991).
18. *Callback,* no. 19 (January 1981).
19. *Callback,* no. 78 (December 1985).
20. *Callback,* no. 95 (May 1987).
21. *Callback,* no. 126 (December 1989).
22. *Callback,* no. 56 (February 1984).
23. *Callback,* no. 19 (January 1981).

Chapter Two

1. "All Things Considered," National Public Radio, WBUR-FM, Boston, October 1990.
2. *Callback,* no. 100 (October 1987).
3. *Callback,* no. 142 (March 1991).
4. Some further intervening text is omitted from the example that is not relevant to the issues at hand.
5. National Transportation Safety Board, "Aircraft Accident Report: Eastern Airlines, Inc., L-1011, N310EA, Miami, Florida, December 29, 1972," report NTSB-AAR-73-14, 1973.
6. *Callback,* no. 28 (October 1981).
7. *Callback,* no. 108 (June 1988).
8. *Callback,* no. 31 (January 1982).
9. *Callback,* no. 4 (October 1979).
10. *Callback,* no. 116 (February 1989).
11. *Callback,* no. 31 (January 1982).
12. *Callback,* no. 114 (December 1988).
13. *Callback,* no. 114 (December 1988).
14. *Callback,* no. 8 (February 1980).
15. *Callback,* no. 3 (September 1979).
16. *Callback,* no. 3 (September 1979).
17. *Callback,* no. 78 (December 1985).
18. *Callback,* no. 78 (December 1985); emphasis added.
19. *Callback,* no. 93 (March 1987).

Chapter Three

1. Steven Cushing, "Not Only *Only,* but Also *Also,*" *Linguistic Inquiry* 9 (1978): 127–32; idem, "Dynamic Model Selection in the Inter-

pretation of Discourse," in *Cognitive Constraints on Communication: Representations and Processes,* ed. L. Vaina and J. Hintikka (Dordrecht: Reidel, 1984); idem, "Two Explanatory Principles in Semantics," in *Matters of Intelligence,* ed. L. Vaina (Dordrecht: Reidel, 1987).

2. *Callback,* no. 45 (March 1983).

3. *Callback,* no. 19 (January 1981).

4. *Callback,* no. 51 (September 1983).

5. *Callback,* no. 52 (October 1983).

6. *Callback,* no. 56 (February 1984).

7. *Callback,* no. 68 (February 1985).

8. *Callback,* no. 47 (May 1983).

9. *Callback,* no. 43 (January 1983).

10. *Callback,* no. 142 (March 1991).

11. *Callback,* no. 46 (April 1983); emphasis added.

12. *Callback,* no. 146 (July 1991).

13. *Callback,* no. 146 (July 1991).

14. *Callback,* no. 82 (April 1986).

15. *Callback,* no. 61 (July 1984).

16. *Callback,* no. 112 (October 1988).

17. *Callback,* no. 100 (October 1987).

18. *Callback,* no. 2 (August 1979); quoted from the *Journal of the Air Traffic Control Association.*

19. *Callback,* no. 20 (February 1981).

20. *Callback,* no. 19 (January 1981).

21. *Callback,* no. 107 (May 1988).

22. *Callback,* no. 112 (October 1988).

23. *Callback,* no. 114 (December 1988).

24. *Callback,* no. 55 (January 1984).

25. *Callback,* no. 156 (May 1992).

26. *Callback,* no. 78 (December 1985).

27. *Callback,* no. 89 (November 1986); emphasis added.

28. *Callback,* no. 90 (December 1986).

29. *Callback,* no. 71 (May 1985).

30. *Callback,* no. 113 (November 1988).

31. *Callback,* no. 105 (March 1988).

32. *Callback,* no. 105 (March 1988).

33. *Callback,* no. 93 (March 1987).

34. *Callback,* no. 47 (May 1983).

35. *Callback,* no. 57 (March 1984); emphasis added.

CHAPTER FOUR

1. Barbara Johnstone, ed., *Repetition in Discourse: Interdisciplinary Perspectives* (Norwood, N.J.: Ablex, 1994).

2. William P. Monan, "'Getting It Straight': The Readback/

Hearback Problem," *Callback*, no. 127 (December 1989).

3. Audiotapes of routine air-ground communications at a major airport.

4. *Callback*, no. 3 (September 1979).

5. *Callback*, no. 80 (February 1986).

6. *Callback*, no. 95 (May 1987).

7. *Callback*, no. 77 (November 1985).

8. *Callback*, no. 52 (October 1983); emphasis added.

9. *Callback*, no. 87 (September 1986).

10. *Callback*, no. 87 (September 1986).

11. *Callback*, no. 65 (November 1984).

12. Some intervening text is omitted. Text is quoted here in the language given in the source.

13. Associated Press, "Avianca Tape Shows Confusion in Cockpit," *Boston Globe*, 28 March 1990.

14. Some further intervening text is omitted from (54) that is not relevant to the issues at hand.

15. National Transportation Safety Board, "Aircraft Accident Report: Eastern Airlines, Inc., L-1011, N310EA, Miami, Florida, December 29, 1972," report NTSB-AAR-73-14, 1973.

16. Roy Wagner, *Symbols That Stand for Themselves* (Chicago: University of Chicago Press, 1986).

17. *Callback*, no. 19 (January 1981).

18. *Callback*, no. 28 (October 1981).

19. *Callback*, no. 86 (August 1986).

20. *Callback*, no. 86 (August 1986).

CHAPTER FIVE

1. *Callback*, no. 8 (February 1980).

2. *Callback*, no. 112 (October 1988).

3. *Callback*, no. 3 (September 1979).

4. *Callback*, no. 22 (April 1981).

5. *Callback*, no. 108 (June 1988).

6. *Callback*, no. 112 (October 1988).

7. *Callback*, no. 28 (October 1981).

8. *Callback*, no. 8 (February 1980); emphasis added.

9. *Callback*, no. 42 (December 1982).

10. *Callback*, no. 71 (May 1985); emphasis added.

11. *Callback*, no. 42 (December 1982); emphasis added.

12. *Callback*, no. 76 (October 1985); emphasis added.

13. *Callback*, no. 42 (December 1982).

14. *Callback*, no. 52 (October 1983).

15. *Callback*, no. 57 (March 1984); emphasis added.

16. *Callback*, no. 57 (March 1984).

17. *Callback*, no. 82 (April 1986).

18. *Callback,* no. 65 (November 1984).
19. *Callback,* no. 57 (March 1984).
20. *Callback,* no. 88 (October 1986).
21. *Callback,* no. 52 (October 1983).
22. *Callback,* no. 5 (November 1979).
23. *Callback,* no. 87 (September 1986).
24. *Callback,* no. 41 (November 1982).
25. *Callback,* no. 17 (November 1980).
26. *Callback,* no. 71 (May 1985); emphasis added.
27. *Callback,* no. 24 (June 1981).
28. *Callback,* no. 22 (April 1981); emphasis added.
29. *Callback,* no. 83 (May 1986).
30. *Callback,* no. 83 (May 1986).
31. *Callback,* no. 19 (January 1981).
32. *Callback,* no. 16 (October 1980).
33. *Callback,* no. 58 (April 1984).
34. *Callback,* no. 64 (October 1984).
35. *Callback,* no. 62 (August 1984).
36. *Callback,* no. 26 (September 1981).
37. *Callback,* no. 19 (January 1981).
38. *Callback,* no. 27 (September 1981).
39. *Callback,* no. 76 (October 1985).
40. *Callback,* no. 76 (October 1985).
41. *Callback,* no. 73 (July 1985).
42. *Callback,* no. 84 (June 1986).
43. *Callback,* no. 22 (April 1981); emphasis added.
44. *Callback,* no. 5 (November 1979).
45. *Callback,* no. 28 (October 1981); emphasis added.
46. *Callback,* no. 105 (March 1988).
47. *Callback,* no. 12 (June 1980).
48. *Callback,* no. 34 (April 1982).
49. *Callback,* no. 49 (July 1983).

Chapter Six

1. *Callback,* no. 37 (July 1982).
2. *Callback,* no. 106 (April 1988).
3. *Callback,* no. 73 (July 1985).
4. *Callback,* no. 112 (October 1988).
5. *Callback,* no. 6 (December 1979).
6. *Callback,* no. 117 (March 1989).
7. *Callback,* no. 158 (July 1992).
8. *Callback,* no. 31 (January 1982).
9. *Callback,* no. 33 (March 1982); no. 74 (August 1985); and no. 94 (April 1987).
10. *Callback,* no. 9 (March 1980).

11. *Callback,* no. 94 (April 1987).
12. *Callback,* no. 35 (May 1982).
13. *Callback,* no. 99 (September 1987).
14. *Callback,* no. 80 (February 1986).
15. *Callback,* no. 41 (November 1982).
16. *Callback,* no. 103 (January 1988).
17. *Callback,* no. 15 (September 1980); emphasis added.
18. Audiotapes of routine air-ground communications at a major airport.
19. *Callback,* no. 154 (March 1992).
20. *Callback,* no. 163 (December 1992).
21. *Callback,* no. 94 (April 1987).
22. *Callback,* no. 4 (October 1979).
23. *Callback,* no. 147 (August 1991).
24. *Callback,* no. 18 (December 1980); emphasis added.
25. *Callback,* no. 36 (June 1982).
26. *Callback,* no. 31 (January 1982).
27. *Callback,* no. 33 (March 1982).
28. *Callback,* no. 9 (March 1980).
29. *Callback,* no. 22 (April 1981).
30. *Callback,* no. 45 (March 1983).
31. *Callback,* no. 40 (October 1982).
32. *Callback,* no. 74 (August 1985).

Chapter Seven

William, P. Monan, "'Getting It Straight': The Readback/Hearback Problem," *Callback,* no. 127 (December 1989).
2. *Callback,* no. 15 (September 1980).
3. *Callback,* no. 70 (April 1985).
4. *Callback,* no. 94 (April 1987).
5. *Callback,* no. 75 (September 1985).
6. *Callback,* no. 14 (August 1980).
7. *Callback,* no. 90 (December 1986).
8. *Callback,* no. 113 (November 1988).
9. *Callback,* no. 41 (November 1982).
10. *Callback,* no. 85 (July 1986).
11. *Callback,* no. 91 (January 1987).
12. *Callback,* no. 91 (January 1987).
13. *Callback,* no. 26 (August 1981).
14. *Callback,* no. 41 (November 1982).
15. *Callback,* no. 100 (October 1987).
16. *Callback,* no. 98 (August 1987).
17. *Callback,* no. 19 (January 1981).
18. *Callback,* no. 71 (May 1985).
19. *Callback,* no. 74 (August 1985).

20. *Callback*, no. 71 (May 1985).

21. *Callback*, no. 93 (March 1987).

22. *Callback*, no. 53 (November 1983); emphasis added.

23. *Callback*, no. 1 (July 1979).

24. *Callback*, no. 50 (August 1983).

25. *Callback*, no. 50 (August 1983).

26. *Callback*, no. 49 (July 1983).

27. *Callback*, no. 31 (January 1982).

28. *Callback*, no. 79 (January 1986).

29. *Callback*, no. 18 (December 1980); no. 30 (December 1981).

30. *Callback*, no. 9 (March 1980).

31. *Callback*, no. 11 (May 1980).

32. *Callback*, no. 39 (September 1982).

33. *Callback*, no. 69 (March 1985).

34. *Callback*, no. 84 (June 1986).

35. *Callback*, no. 77 (November 1985).

36. *Callback*, no. 24 (June 1981).

37. *Callback*, no. 146 (July 1991).

38. *Callback*, no. 155 (April 1992).

39. *Callback*, no. 73 (July 1985).

40. *Callback*, no. 102 (December 1987).

41. *Callback*, no. 103 (January 1988).

42. *Callback*, no. 104 (February 1988); emphasis added.

43. *Callback*, no. 39 (September 1982).

44. *Callback*, no. 72 (June 1985).

45. *Callback*, no. 102 (December 1987).

46. *Callback*, no. 32 (February 1982).

Chapter Eight

1. Audiotapes of routine air-ground communications at a major airport.

2. *Callback*, no. 86 (August 1986).

3. *Callback*, no. 74 (August 1985).

4. *Callback*, no. 112 (October 1988).

5. *Callback*, no. 91 (January 1987).

6. *Callback*, no. 79 (January 1986).

7. *Callback*, no. 14 (August 1980).

8. *Callback*, no. 19 (January 1981).

9. *Callback*, no. 14 (August 1980).

10. *Callback*, no. 42 (December 1982); emphasis added.

11. *Callback*, no. 42 (December 1982).

12. *Callback*, no. 142 (March 1991).

13. *Callback*, no. 87 (September 1986).

14. Audiotapes of routine air-ground communications at a major airport.

15. *Callback,* no. 98 (August 1987).
16. *Callback,* no. 98 (August 1987).
17. *Callback,* no. 98 (August 1987).

CHAPTER NINE

1. *Callback,* no. 81 (March 1986); emphasis added.
2. *Callback,* no. 52 (October 1983).
3. *Callback,* no. 14 (August 1980); emphasis added.
4. *Callback,* no. 19 (January 1981); emphasis added.
5. *Callback,* no. 91 (January 1987).
6. *Callback,* no. 163 (December 1992); emphasis in original.

CHAPTER TEN

1. *Webster's New Universal Unabridged Dictionary,* 2d ed. (New York: Simon and Schuster, 1983).

2. See, for example, Steven Cushing, "Lexical Functions and Lexical Decomposition: An Algebraic Approach to Lexical Meaning," *Linguistic Inquiry* 10 (1979): 327–45; S. L. Tsohatzidis, ed., *Meanings and Prototypes: Studies on Linguistic Categorization* (New York: Routledge, 1990); Mark Aronoff, ed., *Morphology Now* (Albany: State University of New York Press, 1991).

3. See, for example, P. Sells, *Contemporary Theories of Syntactic Description,* CSLI Monograph (Chicago: University of Chicago Press, 1988).

4. The verb-final (b) forms of (182) and (183) are preferred stylistically in Latin, but this is an irrelevant nicety at the present level of discussion.

5. See, for example, Steven Cushing, "Abstract Control Structures and the Semantics of Quantifiers," in *Proceedings of the First Conference of the European Chapter of the Association for Computational Linguistics* (Pisa, Italy, 1983); idem, "Some Quantifiers Require Two-Predicate Scopes," *Artificial Intelligence* 32 (1987): 259–67; idem, "Two Explanatory Principles in Semantics,: in *Matters of Intelligence,* ed. L. Vaina Dordrecht: Reidel, 1987).

6. See for example, Steven Cushing, "Dynamic Model Selection in the Interpretation of Discourse," in *Cognitive Constraints on Communication: Representations and Processes,* ed. L. Vaina and J. Hintikka (Dordrecht: Reidel, 1984); J. Verschueren, ed., *Pragmatics at Issue* (Philadelphia: Benjamins, 1991); idem, ed., *Levels of Linguistic Adaptation* (Philadelphia: Benjamins, 1991); idem, ed., *The Pragmatics of International and Intercultural Communication* (Philadelphia: Benjamins, 1991).

7. See, for example, R. Reichman, *Getting Computers to Talk Like You and Me: Discourse Context, Focus, and Semantics* (Cambridge, MIT Press, 1985); R. W. Ehrich and R. C. Williges, eds., *Human-Computer Dialogue Design* (Amsterdam: Elsevier, 1986); K. Hopper and I. A. Newman,

eds., *Foundation for Human-Computer Communication: Proceedings of the IFIP WG 2.6 Working Conference on the Future of Command Languages* (Rome, 23–27 September 1985) (Amsterdam: North-Holland, 1986); R. G. Reilly, ed., *Communication Failure in Dialogue and Discourse: Detection and Repair Processes* (Amsterdam: North-Holland, 1987).

CHAPTER ELEVEN

1. See, for example, C. P. Robinson and R. E. Eberts, "Comparison of Speech and Pictorial Displays in a Cockpit Environment," *Human Factors* 29, no. 1 (1987): 31–44.

2. Donald L. George, "Taxi To," *Callback,* no. 159 (August 1992).

3. *Callback,* no. 160 (September 1992).

Glossary

Standard Contractions Used in the Examples

AAS   Airport Advisory Service
ALT   altitude
ATA   Airport Traffic Area
ATC   air traffic control
ATIS   Automatic Terminal Information Service
CTAF   common traffic advisory frequency
DME   distance measuring equipment (TACAN compatible)
FAA   Federal Aviation Administration
FL   flight level
F/O   first officer
GA   general aviation
GUMPS   gas, undercarriage, mixture, props
IFR   Instrument Flight Rules
ILS   instrument landing system
IMC   instrument meteorological conditions
MAP   aeronautical maps and charts
MSAW   minimum safe altitude warning
MSL   mean sea level
NORDO   no radio
OM   outer marker, instrument landing system
PA   public address, public announcement
PIC   pilot in command
QNH   altimeter subscale setting to obtain elevation when on the
           ground
REIL   runway end identifier lights
TACAN   UHF Tactical Air Navigational Aid
TCA   terminal control area
TRACON   terminal radar approach control
UHF   ultrahigh frequency
UNICOM   universal communication frequency
VFR   Visual Flight Rules
VHF   very high frequency

From "Contractions," document 7340.1E, Department of Transportation, Federal Aviation Administration, Air Traffic Service.

VOR   VHF omnidirectional radio range
VORTAC   combined VOR and TACAN system (colocated civil VHF
               omnirange/military UHF omnirange with distance
               information)
WX   weather information

Index of Subjects

Index of Problematic Phrases